FR 88

99

IL 89

1990

9 0

16

em is lent
ed will be

A heavy horse towing a tanker-barge.

The Horse on the Cut
Donald J. Smith

Tracking on a barge canal

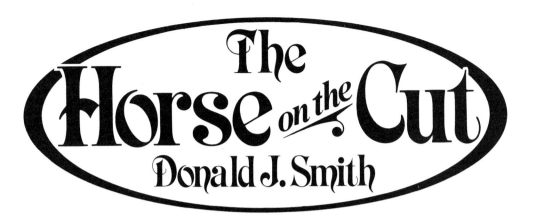

The Horse on the Cut
Donald J. Smith

The story of the
canal horses of Britain

 Patrick Stephens, Cambridge

First published 1982

British Library Cataloguing in Publication Data

Smith, D.J.
 The horse on the cut.
 1. Barges—History
 2. Inland waterway transportation
 —Great Britain—History
 I. Title
 386'229   VM396

 ISBN 0-85059-514-2

Text photoset in 10 on 11 pt English Times
by Manuset Limited, Baldock, Herts.
Printed in Great Britain on 100 gsm
Fineblade cartridge by St Edmundsbury Press,
Bury St Edmunds, Suffolk and bound by
The Garden City Press, Letchworth, Herts,
for the publishers Patrick Stephens Limited,
Bar Hill, Cambridge, CB3 8EL, England.

Contents

Acknowledgements

The author wishes to thank the following for the loan of photographs, and for information or practical help received in compiling this book: Aberdare Library (Curator and staff); The BBC Midland Region; The Boat Museum, Ellesmere Port; *The Birmingham Post and Mail*; M. Brindley; British Waterways Board; T. Conder (Curator of the Waterways Museum); Cynon Valley Borough Library; Hertfordshire Record Office; Alan Hutchison; Kidderminster Library; Lancaster Central Library; P. Lansdell; Jean Lindsay; The Linlithgow Canal Society; *Linlithgow Journal and Gazette*; Manchester Museum; The Mansell Collection; G.D. Moore; The Museum of English Rural Life, University of Reading; Oxford County Library; Pontypridd Public Library; Derek Pratt; *The Scotsman* Publications Ltd; P.M. Smith; Victoria and Albert Museum; Michael E. Ware, FPRS; The Waterways Museum and staff; *Waterways World*; Weybridge Museum; M.G.C. Wheele; Michael Williams; *The Yorkshire Post*.

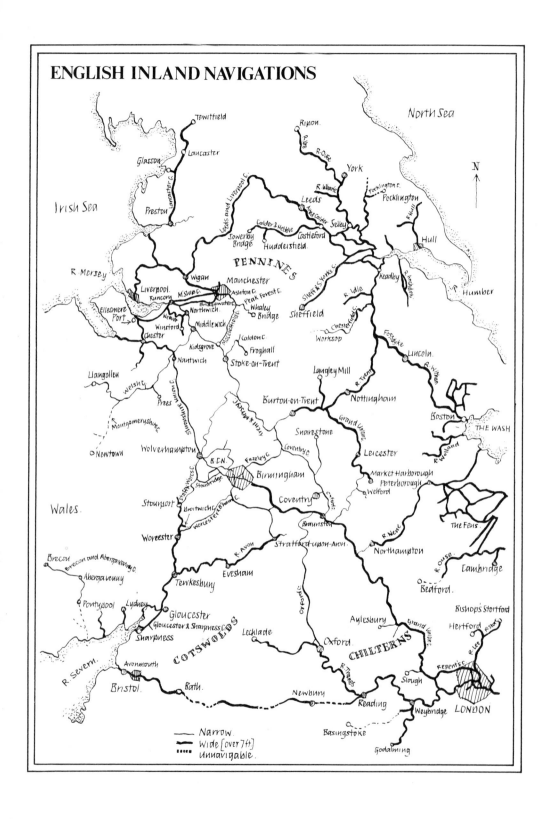

The canal network

The present network of artificial waterways may be divided between ship canals linking inland ports with tidal estuaries, broad canals for barges, and narrow canals over which the once familiar narrow boats worked—between the main cities and industrial centres. This formed the background of horse towage over a period of nearly 200 years, although horses and mules were first used for drawing barges and similar craft over navigable rivers and improved drains from the time of the Roman occupation.

While there is some dispute as to which was the first important canal or artificial cut of modern times, rivers and estuaries were navigated even during the pre-Celtic era, forming water highways when much of the interior was covered with impenetrable forest and swamp. Tracks or roads throughout Britain were unusable at certain periods of the year, at least until the turnpike system of the 18th century, the necessary trade and communications being waterborne, either inland or coastwise. The Celts or Ancient Britons are known to have made extensive use of skin boats such as the coracle and curragh, versions of which were suitable for sea-crossings, coastal trade and traversing shallow streams many miles inland. With the coming of the Romans, drains and dykes were often constructed which served a dual purpose. Their main aim was to drain marshes in low-lying areas, while a secondary purpose was to supplement an improved network of land highways, forming links between natural rivers and inlets, as with the Foss Dyke (joining the lower reaches of the Trent with the East Anglian Wash, via the River Witham).

The great civil engineering works of the Romans were neglected throughout the Saxon and Mediaeval periods of English history, although at certain intervals attempts were made to dredge or scour existing waterways, sometimes by royal decree. The first navigation canal suitable for larger or sea-going vessels was constructed during the reign of Elizabeth I to bypass the lower reaches of the River Exe, between its estuary and the city of Exeter. Navigation of the river itself had been restricted, many years earlier, by the construction of a weir (to serve local corn mills) owned by Isabella de Fortibus, Countess of Devon. This is still known as Countess Weir in her honour. A gate or passage through the weir, suitable for medium-sized craft, was later blocked in 1248 by the powerful Earl of Devon, whose descendants of the Courtney family built a quay at Topsham, further down stream, where all vessels were forced to tranship their cargoes and pay heavy duties for the privilege.

With the decline of the Courtneys from royal favour, during the 16th century, there was open rebellion against their legalised piracy. Proceedings were taken by the Corporation of Exeter to restore the ancient rights of navigation, culminating in an Act to remove obstructions across the river and revive flagging trade. Yet, by this time, the Exe had become unsuitable for the passage of larger craft and John Trew of Glamorganshire was commissioned to make an artificial cut parallel with the river in the vicinity of a watergate in Exeter City. This was begun in 1564 and completed in its original form about two and a half years later. Funds for it were raised by the sale of Corporation plate and by public subscriptions. There were three pound locks, in addition to tide and flood gates, which appear to have been the first of their kind in Britain.

A similar type of navigation, but for smaller craft, was constructed 200 years later in East Lancashire, joining the town of St Helens with the estuary of the Mersey near Widnes. This was known as the St Helen's Canal and it utilised the course of the Sankey Brook, which may be described as an improved section. Constructed between the years 1755 and 1757, with an extension added in 1759, this may be termed the forerunner of the modern canal system, mainly concerned with the distribution of coal and local products. It was still, however, related to the former trade of existing streams and rivers. The first truly independent canal or cut constructed by order of Francis Egerton, 3rd Duke of Bridgewater, was opened in 1761 and named after its founder. This connected underground workings of the Duke's colliery or drift mine at Worsley with the centre of Manchester, and also joined the Mersey at Runcorn (at a slightly later period) and eventually the Leeds and Liverpool Canal via its Leigh Branch. Although the Duke was the main inspiration behind the scheme—having made a study of Continental waterways in early youth—he was assisted on the practical side by his land agent, John Gilbert, and an eccentric genius, James Brindley (1716-1772), a former mill and wheelwright, recommended to the Duke by Gilbert. The main purpose of the Bridgewater Canal was to overcome the combined inefficiency and monopoly of men owning strings of pack horses and committees responsible for earlier river navigations. Many of the navigations had fallen into disrepair despite the heavy tolls levied on their behalf. Once the monopoly was challenged, trade and standards of living improved—especially in urban areas—but prices actually fell.

Throughout the second half of the 18th century men of enterprise and intellect often combined their talents in the promotion of canals and it was after discussions between Erasmus Darwin (the poet, scientist and philosopher) and Josiah Wedgwood (the master potter) with others of like mind, that James Brindley was employed to survey the first great trunk route between the upper Trent and the Estuary of the Mersey, later known as the Trent and Mersey Canal. A national system of waterways eventually extended south west to join the navigable reaches of the Severn and south east, via an Oxford Canal and the Thames, to reach London. This was in the form of a St Andrew's cross and known for many years as the 'Silver Cross', linking London, Liverpool, Hull and Bristol via the estuaries of the Thames, Mersey, Humber and Severn. A shorter cut through the Chilterns was eventually made to London, avoiding delays and uncertainties of navigation on the Thames below Oxford. Other canals crossed the Pennines or served the needs of local industries, as with the tub-boat canals of Shropshire. The last trunk route was the main line of the Shropshire Union Canal, then known as the Liverpool-Birmingham Junction Canal, that made an even more direct contact between Birmingham, the Black Country and a Mersey

The Duke of Bridgewater   James Brindley

outlet, via Ellesmere Port and the Wirral Peninsula. Birmingham had its own internal system of navigations, first constructed by James Brindley and his assistants but later improved by Thomas Telford (1757-1834), serving local mines and factories with short haul or day boats. It was also the terminus for extensive traffic from both London Docks and the northern ports. Being near the centre of England it was at the apex of the silver cross (having a greater mileage of canals than Venice) and was important as a crossing place and in the transhipment of general merchandise to all parts of the country.

During the 1890s the Manchester Ship Canal turned that city into a great inland port for ocean-going vessels, bypassing Liverpool and rivalling the Bridgewater Canal, although it was later controlled by the same authorities. Other canals for barges and larger vessels, rather than boat traffic, cut across the entire breadth of Scotland from east to west, as with the Forth and Clyde Canal and the Caledonian Canal, while the Crinan Canal shortened the westerly sea route round the Mull of Kintyre. In the south west midlands a ship canal between Gloucester and Sharpness reduced the overall length of the navigation, while avoiding shoals, shallows and meanders of the lower Severn, and also reduced the need for shipping and barge traffic to encounter its seasonal bores (or miniature tidal waves) that encroached as far north as a junction with the Avon navigation at Tewkesbury.

Trunk canals of the 18th century, as constructed by Brindley, zig-zagged across country almost like rivers, following natural contours but serving the greatest possible catchment area for trade purposes, while avoiding the difficulty and expense of making tunnels or lock flights. The more experienced and sophisticated engineers of a slightly later period, such as William Jessop (1745-1814) and Thomas Telford, constructed less picturesque but even more impressive canals, cutting a straight line through, rather than round, obstacles, with works that included many aqueducts, tunnels, high embankments and deep cuttings.

Although they brought wealth and prosperity to long neglected areas, the canals were themselves challenged and finally superseded by steam railways. From the mid-19th century many of the canal companies gradually sold out to their commercial rivals, beginning a long period of slump and neglect. The major part of the system was nationalised with the main line railways in 1948, at a time when the waterways were still suffering from wartime shortages and lack of maintenance. Although the Inland Waterways Executive continued to work the more viable freight and mineral haulage sectors for a number of years, it was eventually decided that the major part of the network should be used for recreational purposes and to supply water to industry. The present British Waterways Board still operates barge traffic over some of the industrial canals and rivers, especially in the north east but, further, have a role as guardian of national amenities involving the interests of many thousand pleasure boaters, anglers, ramblers and leisure-seekers. The horse still has a part to play, hauling excursion boats on some of the less widely used waterways, especially those over which preservation societies have a controlling interest, but they have disappeared from the main trunk routes since the end of the Second World War.

Chapter 1

Beginnings

Craft moving over the inland waterways were first propelled by sailing or punting, the latter mainly for short distances. This would apply equally to the early canal and river traffic of Ancient Egypt, China and the primitive waterways of Europe. Haulage from the bank would be necessary when a craft was becalmed or, on river navigations, when encountering shoals, shallows or rapids. Men were used for so-called bowhauling in the ancient civilisations as slave labour before the introduction of draught animals. They were especially useful when the banks were high and it was difficult to construct towing paths, or where there were numerous inlets and marshy places along the river margins. Two legs might scramble where four legs would find it harder to go, although troops using pack mules in jungle and mountain warfare might be inclined to challenge this statement. Much also depended on local custom and the availability of labour. It is more likely, however, that human bowhauliers were associated with shorter routes, while those using animals—especially in later years—would depend on them for longer passages, rather than for traversing places of exceptional difficulty. While it was centuries before some rivers acquired towing paths, these were nearly always built along canal sides, mainly on one bank only of a navigation. In places where traffic was exceptionally heavy there would be towing paths on both sides, as with some of the improved Birmingham navigations of Telford.

The Romans introduced both navigation canals and surfaced roads to Britain, during the period of their occupation (40 AD-410 AD). Their better known waterways, first cut as drains, included the Caer Dyke and The Foss Dyke which formed an important link between Peterborough, Lincoln and the River Trent. The Foss Dyke (now the Fossdyke and Witham Navigations) is still used by modern pleasure craft. The Romans were greatly dependent on mules for all forms of transport, and hauling boats or barges was no exception. These animals were also used as steeds and in agricultural work, so important to the economy of the Empire that books on veterinary matters were mainly devoted to curing sick mules, known collectively as 'mulomedicina' or mule medicine. There were several references to mules drawing canal barges in the writings of Horace, especially in his description of the voyage to Brundusium, appearing in his 15th satire of the first book. One passage describes how the mule was left hobbled to graze or rest at will, in the heat of the day, while the bargee enjoys a well-earned siesta. The number of mules used for towing ranged from singles to pairs and even larger teams depended on the size of the craft involved. Although the Romans made extensive use of mules in Britain, as in other parts of Europe, they were less widely used after their departure from these islands. This latter period corresponds with the neglect of the great transport heritage of the Roman Empire, concerning both roads and waterways.

The waterways of Britain showed gradual signs of revival during the early Middle Ages (often under monastic patronage and enterprise), especially in the Eastern counties, although it is doubtful if mules were again used in large numbers until the mid-18th century. There are records of barge horses used on the inland reaches of the Thames during the Tudor and Stuart periods, also descriptions of bowhauling by gangs of men. It is clear, however, that haulage from the bank was, especially on the broader reaches, an expedient relating to times of drought or parts of the river naturally shallow at most seasons of the year. When barge-masters could rely on wind, tide or current they were much happier to do this than to call upon either men or animals for towing purposes. Where rivers narrowed, however, with an even greater congestion of traffic in proportion to average draught and beam, craft had to be kept moving and many of the so-called 'Western barges' on the Thames were hauled by teams of many horses, some of which may be seen floundering through shallows in water colours and sketches of the artist W.H. Pyne, especially in his *Microcosm* of 1807. As many as 12 horses were frequently recorded for larger vessels, with a further six when an extra barge was taken in tow. The tow ropes are said to have lasted only two or three trips in each direction, costing the barge owners between £10 and £12 (during the mid-18th century), then a considerable sum.

These up-stream or 'western barges' were smaller than those working towards the estuary, with a capacity of between 70 and 80 tons, against a maximum of 146 tons on the lower reaches. Despite the assistance of men, horses and sometimes plough-oxen, borrowed from local farmers, they were often stranded in time of drought and held in the mud for days or weeks at a time. Flushes from the sluices of local millers, further up-stream, were sometimes effective in refloating a vessel but for many years there was great rivalry between millers and bargees so that co-operation was seldom the order of the day. Both navigators and the owners or tenants of water mills claimed to have prior rights regarding ultilisation of the water supply, a contest in which millers—frequently backed by powerful land-owners—were usually successful. Those supporting the barge owners were the merchant class, seldom able to exercise their full legal rights in a feudal society, at least until the great political and social changes during the mid-Tudor period.

A type of flat-bottomed western barge, drawing 16 inches, traded between London and Oxford from the later Saxon period until the mid-19th century. Bowhauliers on the Thames were known as 'halers' or haling men, mainly active until the closing decades of the 18th century. Regular horse towing was not widely used on this river until the turn of the century.

On the River Severn and its tributaries towage was, for many years, the preserve of loutish gangs, perhaps descended from the river pirates and wreckers that haunted the lower reaches—many finding refuge in the Forest of Dean—from the late Middle Ages. They were a rough and ready crew roving the banks and touting for work on the quays of riverside towns, but also raiding farms and cottages, sometimes to steal or plunder but often from sheer devilment. A more disorderly, foul-mouthed group of men would be hard to imagine, confused in the public mind with the bargees themselves, so that long

Bowhauliers negotiating with a trow skipper

afterwards anyone even remotely connected with boat and barge traffic was assumed to be untrustworthy, profane and dishonest. The self-appointed 'captains' or leaders of such rabble bargained with the barge-masters or skippers of trows in taverns (often known as mug houses), hiring the service of their men to the highest bidder, taking part-payment in advance and sealing the contract with a mug of ale or rough cider. Yet even after the most binding agreement it was not unusual for bowhauliers to go back on their word for a few extra pence, from which is derived the old saying 'had for a mug'.

Bowhauling, Wey Navigation, c 1900.

It may be noted that rough cider was a favourite tipple amongst the riverside folk in both Worcestershire and Gloucestershire, many wayside taverns sold little else and were known as cider houses. Perry was also drunk in parts of Gloucestershire, mainly on the west bank, this and cider being far more potent than beer—as then brewed—which may have contributed to the pranks and high spirits of those imbiding large quantities. Time passed slowly for men of low intelligence and, when not sweating at their tow-ropes, having quickly spent their last wages, nothing would be safe from their mischief. The appearance of footloose bowhauliers was as much to be dreaded by local cottagers as the spring floods, when similar evading action would be taken, shutting themselves and their valuables in an upper room until danger had passed. In the meanwhile fruit would be stripped from orchard trees, fowls and even live pigs stolen from the outhouses, hedges flattened and windows broken, leaving a trail of desolation. Bowhauliers were gradually made redundant along the banks of the Severn from the late 18th century with the construction of horse-towing paths introduced by private companies.

A rough towing path may have been stamped-out by the bowhauliers themselves at an earlier period, but very little was planned or engineered before a meeting to discuss this project held by the merchants of Bewdley, Kidderminster and Stourbridge (Worcestershire), eager to petition for such works and to launch a Bill before Parliament. This was in 1761 but it was more than ten years later, after the opening of the Staffordshire and Worcestershire Canal in 1772, that an Act was obtained, its rights of use and construction first exercised on the upper reaches of the river by the Bewdley Bridge and Coalbrookdale Horse-towing Path Company. Eventually there were other

Galton Bridge, Birmingham Canal, showing double towing paths.

Horses in tandem crossing Black Boy bridge on the Wey Navigation.

companies controlling horse towing between Bewdley and Worcester, and Worcester and Gloucester, with very little towing south of Tewkesbury, and a general decline on all parts of the river from the 1870s. Construction work was thorough but slow and it was not until 1812 that a through path was completed to Shrewsbury, then the head of regular navigation. It may be noted that there was navigation over the river to Pool Quay in Montgomeryshire, at certain seasons of the year, but this greatly depended on the level of the water. Railway competition was a serious factor from the mid-19th century, especially with the opening of the Severn Valley Railway in 1862, the last commercial barges reaching Shrewsbury during the same year.

There was still great rivalry between bowhauliers and those concerned with horse towing well into the third decade of the 19th century, with riots along the towing path in 1832 that required the intervention of the regular army, including units of the Royal Scots Greys. Although bowhauling was mainly confined to rivers there was a limited amount of towing by gangs of men on the Thames and Severn Canal and the Stroudwater Navigation, long after it had ceased on other waterways. The exact social position of the bowhauliers is hard to define, especially on the Severn, as, while some were little more than casual labourers, living and sleeping rough, others were from more respectable backgrounds—perhaps ne'er-do-well younger sons—but known to have money invested in river barges or related to owners or skippers of trows. Craft involved in the Severn trade at this period, drawn either by men or horses, were usually barges between 20 and 50 tons burthen or large trows navigating into the Bristol Channel—sometimes to the South Wales Ports—carrying between 40 and 80 tons of cargo, but lesser amounts up-stream from Gloucester. The number of bowhauliers involved, according to the size of the vessel, varied between a mere five or six to ten or twelve.

In the Fenland districts of East Anglia, horses were used for upwards of 300 years, both for hauling single barges and gangs or trains of lighters, of a type once familiar on the Bedford Level. Horse towing paths were long established, at least in rudimentary form, from Essex to Lincolnshire and many of the landscapes of John Constable showed barge horses, often in the care of boys—known locally as 'horse knockers'. They were responsible for driving and often riding the barge horses and were noted for a toughness and vigour without which they could not have survived their harsh conditions. When serving with 'gangs' of lighters they slept in a specially constructed shelter on the third lighter, little better than a dog kennel. They were described as often 'badly treated, badly clothed, bare-footed in all weathers and sometimes under-fed'.

The horses themselves were roughly used and in some places forced to jump stiles along the towing path, these being cheaper to maintain than the original swing gates. This is the subject of Constable's painting *The Leaping Horse,* which often puzzles those unaware of towing path conditions in the area. Although these stiles were not very high, they were serious obstacles to a heavy horse encumbered by harness and towing gear, while the unskilled rider bobbed about on its withers (shoulders) like an overgrown monkey. In wet and slippery weather the stiles still had to be jumped and, although few horses fell at their fences, they were often a mass of cuts and bruises, usually caused by knocking their limbs against the top bars, in addition to suffering galls from wet and badly fitting harness. Sadly these conditions continued until well into the present century and were greatly deplored by Mr H. de Salis in his 1904 edition of *Bradshaw's Canals and Navigable Rivers,* from which the following is quoted: 'In the large group of waterways of the Bedford Level and District, an antiquated substitute for these gates [swing gates] is still in general use in the shape of stiles some as high as 2′7″, over which horses towing [lighters] have to jump, giving themselves frequently nasty knocks in so doing. It is not creditable to the various authorities in the district that such inconvenience to horses is allowed to continue, especially seeing that they stand alone among all the other inland navigations of England'.

In the Fens and Eastern counties there were few roving or turn-over bridges (where a towing path changed sides), and horses were often taken across in specially constructed boats or lighters, known as 'horse boats', not to be confused with boats hauled by horses. They were ferries, shafted or hauled over by ropes, often swim-ended craft like punts, owned by the navigation companies, appearing mainly in East Anglia and on the River Thames. They were last used, however, on the River Trent and the Suffolk Stour. One of these appears in a Constable oil painting known as *The White Horse.* Other types of horse boat, used also by vehicles and pedestrians, were much wider than the average lighter, with a broad, flat deck area surrounded by protective rails or stanchions. These were boarded by means of a gangway let down from either the bows or the side of the craft, broadside-on.

When fenland lighters worked in gangs, trains or runs the last boat in a gang, apart from a small 'cockboat' or pram (rowing boat), would be known as the 'horse boat', used to take the horse across where there was neither bridge nor ferry.

On Constable's River Stour and some of the other waterways of this area

Above *Junction of the Regent's Canal, Paddington.*
Below *Opening a branch of the Ashby Canal, c 1913.*

Left *A detail from* Flatford Mill *by John Constable,* RA.

Below *A horse ferry on the River Severn, c 1930.*

A horse ferry

(Essex and Suffolk), horses were trained to trot ahead of their boat when the towing line was cast off, wait at the end of a short jetty and leap aboard the slatted deck. Where boats or barges worked in pairs, closely chained together like fenland lighters, the horse jumped onto the foredeck of the first boat, perhaps covered with straw to make it less slippery. The boat then drifted across to an opposite jetty where the towing line was reconnected, and the horse scrambled ashore. This was done without delay, a feat of timing and self confidence—worthy of a circus act few animals of equal size could have accomplished.

Nearly all navigations dating from the second half of the 18th century had properly constructed towing paths, used by horses, mules or donkeys but seldom for bow hauling, except on the Thames and Severn Canal, the River Severn and upper reaches of the Thames, as previously mentioned. These towing paths or haling paths (also known as hauling paths or ways) were—on canals—paved and levelled as the responsibility of the canal company. On rivers they were the concern of either the River Board or separate companies concerned only with towing. River towing paths crossed private land and were subject to the laws concerning wayleave. Canal towing paths, enclosed and regarded as canal company property (with private rights of way), were governed by many regulations and bylaws, the latter posted up at frequent intervals. In certain towns, however, the canal side towing path was the only access to a number of houses and factories, widely used for this purpose but also—with limitations—as public footpaths. Under the jurisdiction of the British Waterways Board a permit has to be obtained for regular walking over towing paths.

Chapter 2

Horses, mules, oxen and donkeys

When Mr de Salis wrote his guide to the canals and navigable rivers, first published in 1904, this was after a survey covering several thousand miles in his private (steam-powered) cruiser *Dragonfly*. He claimed that towing mules were then extremely rare, a statement relating to the closing decades of the 19th century. At the time horses accounted for over two-thirds of motive power on the canal system, but were less frequently used on navigable rivers where steam tugs and steam-powered craft in general had rapidly gained control from the mid-19th century. Yet steam power on canals had never been an unqualified success for a number of reasons, perhaps the most telling being the amount of valuable space taken up by the engine, boiler and fuel bunker. The use of steam on canals was also inhibited by limitations on the size of craft passing through locks and bridgeholes. Until the period of the First World War the internal combustion engine was undergoing an experimental phase, which gave the horse a barely disputed monopoly for at least 150 years.

Horses were essentially the English choice, for reasons of climate, temperament and availability; sound economics appearing very low on the list of priorities. In a country such as Britain, naturally favourable for rearing horses, they would be bred in large numbers and their use encouraged to underprop the breeding industry. During the late 18th century a few enlightened industrialists—including the Duke of Bridgewater—also local magnates and country squires, tried to establish breeding centres for the production of mules, which accounted for their use on the inland waterways (in substantial numbers) until the mid-19th century, after which they rapidly dwindled—at least on the main lines. Another supporter of mules at this period was Samuel Skey, a dry-salter of 'Spring Grove', near Bewdley, who was widely involved in the Severn Trade. He not only bred them for work on his home farm and to draw his private carriages, but advocated their use for both road haulage and river or canal towage, claiming this would greatly assist the national economy.

The first boat or barge to traverse the Bridgewater Canal at its opening in 1761, was a type of flat known as *The Young Duke* (named after the third Duke of Bridgewater), drawn by two mules working as a pair (side by side), although in later years they would more likely have worked in tandem (one behind the other). It started from moorings near Barton Aqueduct and appears to have been a family boat steered by the boater's wife while her husband—on the towing path—drove, rather than led, his team, cracking a heavy cart whip. When packet or passage boats were introduced on this line for passenger use, these were horse-drawn as horses were generally faster, although ill-bred types of carthorse used with some of the early craft may well have been forced beyond their normal, sluggish paces.

While the majority of mules were first used in the north of England, especially on the Bridgewater Canal, they often seemed synonymous with poverty rather than prosperity. From the Middle Ages, horses and their use had often been a token of wealth and social advancement, an idea that may have percolated to all sections of the community using draught animals. Even until the third decade of the present century the value of an East Anglian farm was recorded in terms of the number of horses kept on the establishment, those with few or no horses being held in contempt. Although there were always Englishmen willing to put their purses before personal pride, a large number of bargees and boaters (especially the self-employed number-ones) were subconsciously influenced to use horses, when mules or donkeys may well have suited them with greatly increased savings. A number of mules appear to have been used by day boaters on the northern parts of the Staffordshire and Worcestershire Canal, also on the Grand Junction (later Grand Union) Canal— during the 1920s, some of which may have been army surplus from the First World War, but this was also a token of increasing economic depression. It may be noted that from the late 1920s large numbers of boaters were forced to leave the canals through a general decline in trade.

In 1934 the steam (tunnel) tugs, established at Braunston and Blisworth Tunnels on the Grand Union Canal line since the 1870s, were withdrawn due to the sharp decline in horse and mule traffic. A few of the more provident owner-boaters such as Joe Skinner on the Oxford and Coventry Canals, remained faithful to mules until after the Second World War, well into the 1950s. During

A horse and donkeys in Victorian England, towing narrow boats.

A mule and horse in tandem, Grand Union Canal, Watford.

the last few months of its active life (in the revenue-earning sense), the gasboat, *Gifford,* carrying bulk liquids for a Mr Bunford of Shebdon (Shropshire Union Canal—main line), was hauled by a grey mule, perhaps the last in the business (retiring in 1971). The *Gifford* and Joe Skinner's last boat, *The Friendship,* are typical examples of craft drawn by towing animals, now preserved at the Boat Museum, Ellesmere Port, having been restored by experts to their original condition.

There are no available records of oxen being used on British canals or rivers for towing purposes, even though a few seemed to have appeared on French and other Continental waterways—where a horse or mule were occasionally harnessed with an ox or even a cow—if only for short distance hauls. In this connection it may be noted that horses and cattle were sometimes harnessed together as mixed ploughing teams, in rural England, and, in Manitoba and other parts of upper Canada, they were used to draw the 'Red River Carts'. It is probable, however, that river craft stranded at low water in times of drought were hauled free by teams of oxen—in country districts—as large numbers were kept for farm work (even when less popular—in general terms—than horses) until the late 19th century, and may have been more readily available than horses in an emergency.

Herds of oxen and cattle of all kinds were used in the early days of canal construction to help tread-down the clay lining or puddle at the bottom of the canal. They seem to have been driven up and down the dry bed of the canal in large droves, by farm labourers hired for the purpose. The cloven hoofs of these animals made distinctive wedge-shaped patterns (skew-tread) that improved the texture of the puddle, which was a stiff mixture of clay and water. In later years canal employees were issued with special 'puddling boots' the heels of which were carved to resemble cloven hoofs.

Apart from their sluggishness and stolidity most plough oxen were the wrong shape and conformation to make good towing animals, except when time was of little importance. Squat, powerful at the fore-end, yet often too near the ground, most oxen had to wear a special kind of harness, working in pairs and pushing against a neck-yoke, fixed to a centre-beam or draught pole at an angle of about 25 degrees, for which there would be insufficient room on most towing paths. It may be noted that a rangy type of beast with longer legs could wear a form of harness normally associated with draught horses—including neck collar, breeching and pad-saddle—but would have to be specially selected from those found in such countries as the United States of America, South Africa and Australia, which have large numbers of surplus cattle in open range conditions. With modern breeding trends towards the more compact carcass it would be increasingly difficult to find such animals in Britain, at least from the second half of the 19th century.

Mules had much in their favour as towing animals or beasts of burden and are undergoing a revival for farm work in parts of the United States of America, although some misguided experts (shortly after the Second World War) predicted that they would soon become extinct or no longer bred in significant numbers. A mule is the offspring of a horse and a donkey, the male or jack being the donkey and the female or mare being the horse. The less frequent cross between a male horse or stallion and a female donkey or jenny, is known as a hinny or a jennet. The jennet, in this case, should not be confused with a small riding horse of the Middle Ages (of the same name and spelling), much lighter than the average charger, war horse or hunter and frequently ridden by ladies. In all cases the offspring takes after the male for looks and the female for strength. Technically the hinny or jennet is not a true mule and although more like a horse in appearance, is comparatively weaker than its cousins of the opposite mating pattern, being very little in demand except (at one time) for light cartage work in the peat bogs of Ireland.

The real mule, usually, but not always, sterile, is in some ways better than either of its parents, exhibiting—apart from coarser looks and the inability to breed—greater courage, stamina and powers of endurance. It is certainly less prone to disease than either horse or donkey, having the firm hoofs and sure-footedness of the donkey, combined with the superior strength of the horse.

A mule   'Dolly', mule owned by Joe and Rose Skinner

Relative to its size and the amount it normally eats, it is nearly always stronger than the horse, in proportion, and frequently lives to a much greater age. While few horses live beyond 20 to 25 years and are unfit for the hardest work long before this age is reached, the mule may reach 40 and upwards, sound in wind and limb. Regarding food, it eats sparingly and is seldom greedy for fodder or water at any season, seeming to have an inbuilt sense of moderation. Mules are, however, independent and difficult to handle without the right sort of understanding. Where a horse may be frightened or beaten into submission by an unfeeling owner, the mule tends to fight back with open rather than sly agression. It will not only kick backwards like a horse, but sideways like a cow and forwards like a man, its forward kick being the most dangerous of all. If well-handled, however, the mule is no danger either to its owner or the general public and may seem the mildest of creatures.

Both Joe Skinner and his wife Rose were animal lovers in the better sense of those much abused words, knowing how to behave towards their mules and getting the best out of them. The author has frequently seen *The Friendship* passing Fenny Compton Wharf on the Oxford Canal, Dolly the mule moving at a swift pace and Joe keeping-up at the rear between a walk and a run, his jacket collar turned against the rain and the brim of a battered trilby hat running like a waterspout. From time to time he would give a light tap on her hind quarters, accompanied by a cheery word or clack of the tongue that would have kept her going forever. Unfortunately, Dolly, nearing old age, caught a chill and died after falling into the canal in cold weather, which further hastened the retirement of her master and mistress.

Joe and Rose worked their craft from collieries on the Coventry Canal such as Griff, Pooley Hall and Newdigate, down to the terminal basin at Oxford, from the 1920s. During the period between the world wars they worked two boats, usually in tandem, these being *The Friendship* and *The Elizabeth,* both built at Sephton's yard, Hawkesbury Junction (also known as Sutton Stop). The boats were hauled by two mules also in tandem—'Dolly' and 'Dick'—crewed by Joe, Rose and her brother. *The Friendship* usually off-loaded at the wharf of King

A mule, eating as he walks.

'Dolly' with The Friendship, *Oxford Canal, 1958.*

and Company while *The Elizabeth* tied-up at the Co-operative Coal Wharf. When the terminal basin was closed and filled-in—to be used as the site for Nuffield College—two years before the Second World War, *The Elizabeth* was sold to Barlows but *The Friendship* was retained for regular commercial runs, serving a radiator factory, Banbury power station and later a dairy at Banbury, until 1959. *The Friendship* was launched in 1925. Other boaters had often councilled the Skinners to give up their mules and invest in a motor boat, but neither were keen on this project, making out that a good mule or pony was far less trouble than a 'motor' and, in the long run, much cheaper.

Whatever the failings of the horse may have been on the towing path, it was of greater actual, if not comparative, strength than donkey or mule. This was combined with a more tractable nature and usually greater willingness to co-operate than might be found in either mules or donkeys. Odd examples might seem stupid or vindictive but such failings are usually the result of constant abuse rather than inbred agression or bad-temper for their own sakes. The tolerance of the horse for ill-treatment is usually of a high order, although breaking point may be reached with even the mildest creatures. On the whole a good horse is one of nature's gentlemen, knowing how to behave himself although not devoid of a sense of humour and capable of sorting out the impostor and incompetent from the expert and trust-worthy. It is often said that horses of certain colours are more reliable and even-tempered than others, with bays, browns, greys and piebalds (black and white in patches) having a better reputation—in general terms—than chestnuts, duns, roans and skewbalds (brown and white). This is partly folk-law and superstition although some colours have always been better liked than others, meaning that unusual or less popular types have sold cheaper and perhaps fallen into the wrong hands at an early age, and have reacted against contempt and partiality in the most obvious way possible. Horses, like most other creatures, reflect their treatment and surroundings, those handled with good-natured firmness being more reliable and co-operative than others treated to alternate bullying and neglect.

Just over 15 hands high was considered a good average for a boat horse (1 hand = 4 inches), but some horses pulling barges may have been up to 17 or 18 hands. The majority seen on British waterways were either mares or geldings.

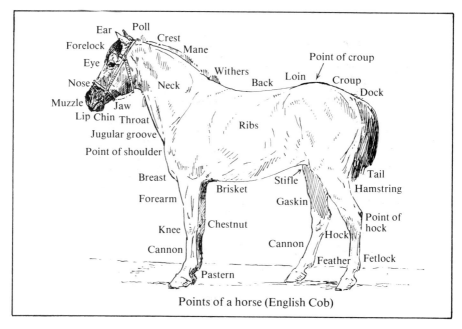

Points of a horse (English Cob)

Stallions or 'entires', being more wilful, were rarely used for draught purposes, especially in England. Although stallions were sometimes ridden or driven in Continental Europe, this does not automatically imply superior horsemastership but a more careless attitude towards life and property. While handling a highly mettled entire had a certain panache for the individual concerned, commercial owners in a country dominated (at the height of its prosperity) by the shop-keeper mentality, would incline against needless risk, prompted as much by economy as altruism.

There was no particular type or breed of horse used for towing purposes, although—with certain exceptions—it is probable that the majority were far from being the youngest, most active or least blemished of their kind. Most boaters and bargees, however, valued a horse that seemed mentally alert and quick to learn. A lot depended on the individual boater or haulage company, concerning expenditure and policy. While some were inclined to look for better quality animals and treat them well—at least in their prime—expecting a high standard of work over an extended period, others bought run-down beasts (old screws) very cheaply and drove them almost to death on the understanding that there were plenty more of the same sort when replacements were needed.

The life story of even the best-bred horse was often a tragedy, passing through phases of hard work but fair treatment, to labour beyond its strength, in the hands of men too poor or unfeeling to consider its needs, ending with a period of sheer drudgery and death in the traces or being sold for dog food. Only the lucky ones would be given rest and semi-retirement, with a merciful end when they became too old for the lightest work, rather than sold out of service to a fate many times worse than death. Perhaps the finest horses on the canals and the best cared-for, were connected with the railway boatage services, hauling so-called 'station boats', up to the period shortly after the Second World War. Railway horses were usually bought by experts about the age of six,

Above *A heavy horse of a type used on the northern canals.* **Below** *A heavy horse, towing on the Regent's Canal, London.*

when they were already well-broken and capable of hard work; few were acquired after the age of seven and a half.

The largest and heaviest horses on the inland waterways were used for river rather than canal haulage, although some of this type were also seen on the canal network, mainly towing barges and lighters on broad or barge canals. They were frequently used in the London area and on the lower reaches of the Grand Union Canal, towing anything from narrow boats (although these were comparatively rare and seldom seen—drawn by heavy horses—north of Uxbridge) to much larger flats, barges and lighters. Such heavyweights were favoured on some of the Fenland waterways, the Basingstoke Canal, the Bridgewater Canal, the Leeds and Liverpool Canal, the Calder and Hebble Navigation, the Aire and Calder Navigation, and also on the rivers Lee, Soar, Stort, Severn, Wey, Suffolk-Stour and Trent. They may be defined as shire types rather than shires, as it is unlikely that more than a few would have found their way into the stud books of the breed society. They may have been a cross between any of the four main breeds of heavy draught horse found in this country, with an intermingling of less distinguished blood. It may be noted, however, that until the early part of the 20th century there would have been little or no influence from the Percheron, now a partly Anglicised French breed, which was scarcely known in Britain until the First World War.

The shire type, if not the pure bred shire, was an ideal barge horse, especially for slower, heavier traffic. It represented one of the most popular and available types of draught animals in Britain, especially in the Midlands, Home Counties, Lancashire and the Welsh Borders. During the Victorian era even its faults (great height and hairy legs) were considered virtues, at least in the show ring. Yet, in its early days, although still fairly tall, it was more compact and stocky than a type beginning to emerge between the world wars. A docile and even-tempered beast, moving at a slow-deliberate pace, it was not perhaps the best sort on which to rely in an emergency, when a sudden change of direction or burst of speed was needed. Teams of shires hold world records for their ability

A Shire

Above *A shire horse hauling a narrow boat, c 1920.* **Below** *Barge horses at Addlestone (Shire types) Wey Navigation, 1950s.*

to move weights and are by far the largest and most powerful breed on average, if not actually the largest known horses as individuals.

The true shire is said to have descended from the 'great horse' of England, used as a knight's charger during the later Mediaeval period when arms and armour were at their heaviest. It charged at a slow trot and was more like a miniature tank than a war horse of either earlier or later periods, trained to lash out with its hoofs when surrounded and carrying its own body-armour. With the widespread use of gunpowder and the improvement of handguns there was a change in military tactics so that heavy horses were no longer needed on the battle-field, except to haul the larger type of howitzer or siege-gun (which latter it continued to do until replaced by steam traction-engines towards the end of the First World War). They were soon switched to agricultural work and general haulage purposes, replacing oxen where greater speed and activity was needed—plus power, also for reasons of show and display, as previously mentioned. The shire might be slow and lumbering but was always quicker and more agile than plough-oxen and made a fine spectacle, especially when decked-out with brasses, ribbons and harness bells.

The breed was greatly improved during the mid-18th century by Robert Bakewell of Dishley. The best shires were about 17 hands high, although the mare was slightly smaller and modern types may be upwards of 18 hands, which latter is impractical in many ways and difficult for harnessing or grooming. Characteristics were the mass of fetlock or feather extending from heels to hocks and from pasterns to knees, a well-ribbed up body or barrel, deep neck and shoulders, high carriage of the head, long but fine ears, a long face and slightly arched or Roman nose. In later years the breed society ordained that only certain colours would be encouraged or acceptable, the ideal being a bay, brown or dark colour.

Right *Ex-riding horse type used for boatage on the Grand Union Canal.*
Below *A grey mare from the Leeds and Liverpool Canal.*

Greys, apart from some darker dapple-greys, have never been popular with horse-keepers, especially with larger horses, as they show up the slightest marks and stains by contrast. Grey horses might therefore be offered cheaper than coloured or darker specimens and readily available to the less fussy or fashion-conscious barge owner. During the early 1960s the author recollects seeing a magnificent grey of the shire type, hauling rubbish boats on the Birmingham Navigations, having the appearance of an ex-railway draught horse.

In horseman's parlance there are no white horses, only greys and creams. The cream horse is now very rare and was originally either an Hanoverian carriage horse (used to pull the Royal State Coach of England, before being replaced by more patriotic Windsor Greys), or a circus horse performing without harness or rider in so-called liberty acts. The cream was also a favourite drum horse in mounted or cavalry bands. Many creams were albinos and had pink eyes and nostrils. A grey or cream horse with leopard-like spots (sometimes only a few of these) is known as an Appaloosa, favoured in North America as a special breed. They are rare in Britain although one was seen hauling a passenger boat on the Llangollen Canal during the summer of 1980.

The heavy draught horse of Scotland, widely used in the Border areas of Northern England and in Northern Ireland (also in countries of the British Commonwealth settled by people of Scots descent), was the Clydesdale. Descended from imported Flemish stallions crossed with native (lowland) mares, it was established as a separate breed during the second half of the 18th century. This was both a town and country horse, equally at home on farms of the Central Lowlands and in the busy streets of mining, dockland and industrial areas, responsible for hauling barges or scows on the Forth and Clyde Canal and the Glasgow Union Canal. It was not quite so tall as the shire but more rangy for its size and comparatively longer in the leg. It has an air of great alertness and is a much quicker mover than the shire but also of less sound temperament. They were usually bays, browns or blacks and most would have

Single horse towing a pair of narrow boats on the Grand Union Canal near Lady Chapel's Wharf.

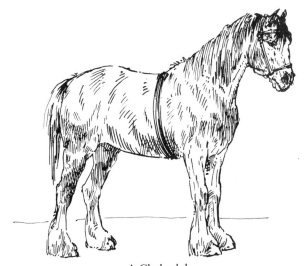

A Clydesdale

considerable white markings such as stockings on the lower limbs and stars, splashes or flashes on head or face. Having a brisk, lively action they needed a brisk, lively person to tend and handle them and were not considered a horse for the novice in stables or the older person lacking in agility and long experience. Some have been crossed with shire stock and the two once-divergent breeds are now closer together, although the original shire may have been more like a large Suffolk Punch, but with a greater amount of fetlock.

The Suffolk Punch, as the name implies, was a native of the southern part of East Anglia, and may have hauled barge traffic on the Chelmer and Blackwater Navigations, the Stowmarket Navigation and on the Suffolk Stour. It was hardy and clean-limbed, but slightly lower and nearer the ground than either the shire

A Clydesdale barge horse.

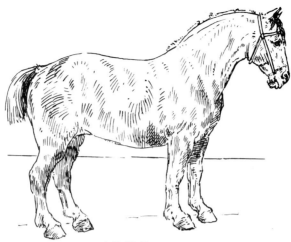

A Suffolk Punch

or Clydesdale. This proved a great advantage in boat or barge hauling and agricultural work, although better for ploughing than for carting. The shorter legs and sturdy body had a low centre of gravity and obtained greater purchase over its load than would have been possible with taller, leggier types. Even the name Punch means compact and powerful, giving the impression of great energy, like a balled fist. It lives longer, on average, than the shire, and other heavy breeds, thriving on less food. Apart from toughness and strength it could muster a fairly swift trot and some were even used, in hilly districts, as heavy coach or carriage horses, and also to breed hunters. Colour was a light to dark chestnut with a lighter coloured mane and tail. A darker and even more attractive type—almost bay—has died out since the Second World War.

The Percheron was originally a French breed that greatly impressed British farmers serving in France during the First World War, also the Ministry of Agriculture and the War Department. Others were brought to Britain by the

A Percheron

Ponies used for towing on the Grand Union Canal at Berkhampstead, 1905.

American and Canadian armed forces, ideal for drawing both field guns and supply wagons. They may be the most widely distributed breed of heavy draught horses in the world—even today—especially favoured in the United States and Canada, until a recent fashion in the USA for Belgian draught horses. Even now fair numbers are being exported to Japan where they are valued by the small farmer and further used for a type of cross-country harness racing (pulling slides or sledges), which is a growth sport in this part of the Far East. It is a sturdy, willing, yet finely made horse, arguably the most beautiful of the heavy breeds, having a combination of warm-blooded Arab stock and descent from some of the best cold-blooded draught lines of northern Europe. The stallion is about 16 hands 3 inches high with the mare an inch or so shorter at the withers, making them appear mid-way between the shire and the punch. Grey, black and slate-blue are the most favoured and typical colours although bays and chestnuts are sometimes seen abroad, not favoured by the English breed society. While having a little more feather or fetlock than the punch, it is almost clean-limbed, with good hard bone and hoofs.

Shires in particular, although appearing robust, were less adaptable to extremes of weather and climate than other breeds. The shire type, with an excessive amount of long hair around its feet and legs, tended to harbour dirt and damp that led to a number of complaints almost unknown to other horses, the worst of which was known as itchy heels. The larger animals, upwards of 18 hands high and weighing a ton apiece, found difficulty in passing under low bridges or through tunnels with towing paths—also in meeting other horses of equal bulk. On river navigations, on some broad canals and in dockland areas, however, the towing paths were broader than on most narrow canals and hump-backed bridges, with low clearance, and were either non-existent or few and far between.

When a heavier draught horse would be needed on the narrow or boat canals, this was one of the smaller or nondescript types. A large number working over

Horse towing on the narrow canals

Boat horse, vanner-type

the Staffordshire and Worcestershire Canal were of the so-called 'vanner' type or half-legged horses, having a moderate amount of feather or fetlock on their limbs and being a cross between a small carthorse or the shire type and an English or standard cob. These were used by common carriers to pull the heavier delivery vans through city streets, up to, during and after the Second World War—until the mid-1950s. They were fairly hardy and withstood extremes of weather much better than the larger draught horses, and also had a livelier gait and quicker paces. It was noticeable, however, that the nearer one came to the Black Country and Birmingham areas, the more likely one was to find smaller horses of the cob-type on the towing paths, a few no larger than well-made ponies. The definition of a pony is a small horse of or under 14 hands, while a cob is a slightly larger animal or cross between a pony and a full-sized horse.

Cobs were widely used by farmers and small tradesmen, especially for market work and country or suburban deliveries. They were long recognised as a special breed as there was a standard cob and the even more attractive and versatile Welsh cob (frequently seen on the Brecknock and Abergavenny Canal). An Irish cob was well-known until the late 19th century, but seems to have died out, like the Welsh carthorse and the Yorkshire coach horse, during the period between the world wars. Cob, like punch, is both a noun and an adjective, describing something compact, handy and useful. All types showed great courage and endurance, able to haul a good weight for their size and frequently used as a dual purpose animal for riding and driving, especially by countrymen, novices and the elderly. Their mild temperament made them ideal for the inexperienced, while they have always had a reputation for sure-footedness, both great advantages in the canalside context. Their legs were usually short but sturdy for the size of their bodies, the conformation being fairly close to the ground but not too low. This made them suitable for squeezing through or under difficult places, of which there were many on the older parts of the Birmingham and Black Country canal network, especially on the Brindley line.

At various intervals both canal companies and individual owner-boaters attempted to up-grade and improve their studs. Horses owned by the railway companies, the Bridgewater Canal Company (especially in later years) and the Shropshire Union Canal Company, however, were nearly always the best of their kind. Owner-boaters tended to buy at the lower end of the market but some were fortunate to acquire the services of ex-carriage horses or even ex-race horses, cast from their aristocratic surroundings for a minor fault or blemish that in no way prevented them from putting in a good day's work on the towing paths. It says much for equine blood and breeding that even in reduced circumstances the blood horse (of thoroughbred descent) showed a vigour and keeness for the task-in-hand that put other horses to shame. Such horses on the canals were so fast and willing, even with a full load, that it was difficult to keep up with them. Sir George Head in his 'Home Tour' of 1835, remarked that many horses on the Goole Canal in East Yorkshire were near thoroughbred, also that aged, high-bred hunters were used on the Carlisle Canal, kept in high condition.

Private barges and inspection craft may have been drawn by the better type of coach or carriage horse, including the Yorkshire Coach Horse and the Cleveland Bay, both bred in East Yorkshire and County Durham, although the former died out during, or shortly after, the Second World War. They both represented a superior type although the Cleveland Bay was slightly heavier and longer in the back and loins, and was between 15.3 and 16 hands high.

Donkeys, working in pairs or tandem, were formerly confined to the Worcester and Birmingham Canal or other waterways of the West Midlands (connecting at some point with the River Severn), including the Stroudwater Navigation and the Droitwich Canals, but were also found—to a limited extent—on the Shropshire Union Canal. At one time a fair number of donkeys

A donkey

Above *Three donkeys towing a barge, Gloucester and Sharpness Canal.*

Right *A rare example of a donkey wearing brasses (facepiece), c 1910.*

worked from a base at Trevor on the Welsh Section of the 'SUC'. Some were even photographed, earlier in the present century, crossing the famous Pontcysyllte Aqueduct, near Llangollen. In France large donkeys, sometimes up to 15 hands, worked on the Canal lateral de la Loire, but often paired with a horse or mule—in later years a horse and mule would be a more frequent sight. Many donkeys in Britain, also known as asses, were imported from the South of Ireland via the Port of Bristol, and used in the West Midlands, especially the Severn Valley, for all types of draught purposes.

Small, handy, yet hard-working, the donkey usually lived to a ripe old age. Like the mule it was much hardier than the horse and less particular about its food and drink, both as to quantity and quality. Two donkeys might be used in place of a single horse or mule, taking up very little room on the towing paths and, where there were tunnels without towing paths, taken into the boat rather than over the top. It may be noted that many tunnels had special horse paths over the summit, and while most horses, mules and donkeys were sensible enough—after training—to find their own way along these, bylaws insisted that they should be led from portal to portal in case attempts were made to steal or molest them. Sir George Head, writing during the 1830s, quoted that 6d (old money) was charged for leading an animal over the top at Standedge Tunnel (Huddersfield Narrow Canal) and 1/- (12 pence old money) for legging a light weight or empty boat through the tunnel. Donkeys were sure-footed with extremely hard hoofs, a characteristic handed down to the majority of draught mules—which meant that a number were never (or rarely) shod. Experts might

A typical boat horse on the Coventry canal, c 1950.

cavil at this and many donkeys were shod at regular intervals, there being special donkey-sized shoes, but a large proportion went unshod, which may have seemed a worthwhile economy to the more greedy or less prosperous owner-boaters.

It appears that the Worcester and Birmingham Canal was far from being the most humane setting in which to find towing animals of any sort. A number of the unfortunate beasts were hired or loaned to boaters by the navigation company and it is widely acknowledged that, where such creatures frequently changed hands and are hired rather than owned, they are likely to be less well treated than animals for which their owners take total responsibility. Yet some became greatly attached to their donkeys and there is even a story—on the Coventry Canal—of a man owning a pair by whom they were sometimes given a ride in the boat (the man bowhauling), if he thought they seemed tired and over-worked. It is worth noting that while some boaters and canal folk term all beasts of draught and burden 'animals' (pronounced 'hanimals'), others reserved this name for donkeys only. The average British donkey was well under 12 hands high, coloured grey or brown but usually grey. Unlike the horse it had a tufted or cow-tail.

Many donkey boaters on the Worcester line preferred to sleep in the stable rather than on the boat. At Hanbury Wharf they were made to pay in advance, then locked in with a lantern or stump of candle. Otherwise they would let in their friends for free lodging and stabling.

Like the mule and the cob, the donkey was able to stand up to rough weather of all kinds, although it had a natural preference for warmer conditions. Its main disadvantage was a rare but sudden inclination to balk or jib. In relation to draught animals this means coming to a full-stop for no apparent reason. With a donkey it was a case of 'so far and no further', perhaps for a matter of hours. While mules were known to jib it was easier to lure them forward by offering a handful of oats, a carrot or even damp earth. A balking horse might be coaxed or beaten into further action but donkeys gave the impression of resisting anything short of a minor explosion. Explanations are that donkeys were intelligent enough to know just how much work they were capable of doing in a given time, needing a fair share of rest. Others claim that donkeys, even more than horses or other domestic animals, were aware—by a rare instinct—of impending danger and anything strange or unusual, refusing to budge until the threat of danger, perhaps unseen by the owner, had passed.

Chapter 3

What they did

Part I

While a single pack horse, once the commonest beast of burden in Britain, would carry a weight of 2 cwt, slung in panniers on either side of its body, the same horse might be expected to pull well over a ton in a four-wheeled wagon on a good road and 10 tons on rail or tram tracks. Yet, because of the buoyancy of water, which in a still water navigation would offer very little resistance from flow or current, a horse could haul upwards of 80 tons by boat or barge. This should have made bank-towing over canals the cheapest form of transport ever devised but does not take into account factors of general upkeep and initial outlay. Canals are often more expensive to construct than roads or railways but much depends on local conditions, especially with regard to maintenance and water supply.

Although, in some respects, complimentary to steam power, the horse stood very little chance when challenged by the more efficient internal combustion engine, both on and off the waterways. Speed and time-saving have become factors of great importance during the 20th century and, although many of the bulk cargoes were stock-piled and did not have to be delivered promptly, perishable goods were always better for saving even a few hours. Here again the internal combustion engine for power boats was an advantage, taking-up far less room and man-power to operate than craft with steam-driven machinery, the larger engines and fuel bunkers of which reduced cargo space. By working at full-throttle the same sized motor boats could do more work in a given time than horse boats and, while in good order, were tireless. Those late in the day to mechanise were, except on certain branch canals or secondary lines, unable to compete and were forced out of business. There remained, however, strongholds of commercial horse and mule towing up to the late 1960s. Even during the 1980s a single horse, owned by 'Caggy Stevens', plies the Birmingham Canal Navigations, while horses are still used for towing excursion and pleasure craft in remoter parts of the country where towing path conditions allow.

Yet despite the obvious advantages of powered craft, the introduction of screw-driven vessels led to running down, rather than boosting, commercial traffic (in the long term), especially on narrow waterways or boat canals. The throbbing propellers of motorboats and tugs, especially those working at maximum speeds, began to accelerate the erosion of banks and towing paths, making them harder to use by the remaining horses, while the constant slippage added problems of silting-up at a time when little money could be spared for dredging. Maintenance was further handicapped by acute manpower shortages during and after the Second World War.

Even after the nationalisation of the major waterways in 1948, a few horses pulled single boats on short or intermediate hauls over the Oxford, Ashby, Coventry and Birmingham Canals. These were mainly used for minor sub-contracts and irregular trips for which the larger operators would not be able to tender for economic reasons.

A minimal amount of repair work has to be kept up on all canals, even when abandoned by ordinary traffic and retained only for drainage or water supply purposes. In many areas the work-boats or flats continued to be horse hauled well into the 1950s and early 60s. It was also possible to see horses used for towing (especially non-powered butties of a working pair) through lock flights, in the Birmingham and Wolverhampton areas and at Audlem on the Shropshire Union Canal, some time after the majority of horse boats had disappeared. Where narrow locks were only wide enough for one boat at a time this would save considerable energy and man-power otherwise wasted in bowhauling between contiguous lock chambers.

At Runcorn, on the Bridgewater Canal, a stable of magnificent shire horses was kept until the end of the Second World War, to haul craft through locks from the lower level of the tidal Mersey. However, beyond the top lock, haulage by horses gave way to steam tugs, which were introduced during the early 1870s, and diesel tugs (from the 1920s). Most of the local traffic consisted of special flats or 'Dukers' (named after the Duke of Bridgewater, founder and first owner of the Canal) which were unpowered craft working over both canal and tideway, needing two horses per fully laden craft. On the long-defunct Carlisle Canal (closed to through traffic in 1853) horses were used for towing sea-going vessels from the tidal Solway or Solway Firth at Port Carlisle, to a basin in the centre of Carlisle City, 11¼ miles distant. Some were merely used, as at Runcorn, for working craft through sea-locks while others—known as 'trackers'—were ridden along the towing paths, their owners touting for work and rendering assistance wherever needed.

Horse haulage on the Leeds and Liverpool Canal continued until 1955. The last horse-hauled craft was owned by H. and R. Ainscough, grain merchants and millers of Parbold and Burscough. This was drawn by a grey shire horse, that also made its way on to the Bridgewater Canal via the Leigh Branch. Most of the Leeds and Liverpool Canal craft were so-called 'short boats', intended to work through sections of the waterway where locks were shorter but wider than on the narrow canals. They were usually all-wooden family boats with transom sterns, employed in the coal trade or as general carriers. Horse towing on this line was challenged by powered craft, especially steam boats, as early as the 1880s, but steam engines—with attendant boilers and fuel bunkers—took up most of the cabin space in the stern part of each vessel, so that horse-drawn craft were more popular for family boating. The Leeds and Liverpool Canal remained a pocket of horse towing, also of steam boats, until the period shortly after the Second World War.

Humber and Yorkshire Keels (some also working on the lower reaches of the Trent), the double-ended barges once so familiar on navigations connected with the Humber and Yorkshire Ouse, were mainly sailing craft, especially working down-stream and on estuarine waters. When proceeding inland, however, (their masts and sails kept in store at various places along the route) they were towed by horses hired for the purpose, at least until the period between the world wars. Keels were of various sizes according to the routes over which they worked. Some smaller types plied as far inland as the Calder and Hebble Navigations and were horse towed for at least half their journeys. They were later known as 'West Country Barges' or 'Vessels', not to be confused with 'West Country Barges' on the Thames, which were also horse hauled for many years. The larger keels were up to a capacity of 100 tons and needed at least two horses to pull them, working in tandem, although only one good horse was required for smaller craft. At one time they were all-wooden barges, the keels noted for their highly varnished exterior surfaces, although later types were of all-steel or iron construction. Men hiring out horses for inland towing over the Yorkshire waterways—above Goole—were known as 'horse marines'.

On the Grand Junction Canal (later the Grand Union Canal) there were large numbers of horses of all types, and a few mules, until the mid-1930s, after which they were replaced by working pairs (boats), powered by internal combustion engines in the leading craft. A steel or composite boat (part wood and part metal, usually with an elm bottom), known as a motor-boat, would tow an all-wooden butty or former horse boat, the rudder or ram's head often decorated with the tail of a grey horse, said to bring good luck. On the lower reaches of the same navigation, south of Uxbridge, the large number of barges and lighters towed by heavy horses until the early 1960s were gradually replaced by small tractor units from the mid-1950s. It is interesting to note, especially by those regarding the horse as a stupid animal, that many of the first tractors were yanked into the water by the pull of the following boat and the driver's lack of 'horse sense'.

The magnificent Wey Barges, owned by William Stevens and Sons of Guildford and Weybridge, with a capacity of 80 tons, operated over the Wey Navigation and Godalming Canal until 1969—some reaching London Docks via the Thames—and were horse hauled until 1960, having two shire horses per boat or barge, worked in tandem. Similar barges also worked over the adjacent Basingstoke Canal until the 1940s.

The most familiar craft to be drawn by towing animals, were the narrow or monkey boats (also known as 'long boats' in the West Midlands and West of England), of roughly 72 ft length but slightly under 7 ft beam. These included open boats for minerals and merchandise and enclosed tankers for cargoes of bulk liquids. Draught of the average narrow boat was 8 in to 11 in empty. The tankers were often known as 'gasboats' because they transported large quantities of vile-smelling gas water, the largest number of these owned and operated by Thomas Claytons (Oldbury) Limited, Oldbury being a Worcestershire town on the outskirts of the Black Country, served by the Birmingham Canal Navigations. Boats of this latter type, but slightly larger dimensions, also worked over the Bridgewater Canal and other northern waterways, known as 'Horse Floats'.

Horse boats of any type usually carried a spare nose or feed can on the stern deck of the main cabin or shelter (stern cabin), while with some craft, especially in the West Midlands, the towing mast near the fore-end could be angled to one side (usually when a boat was empty and high in the water) to prevent scraping bridgeholes. On horse- or mule-drawn gasboats there would be a feed barrel and tent-like erection containing fodder, at the rear of the towing mast, known as a

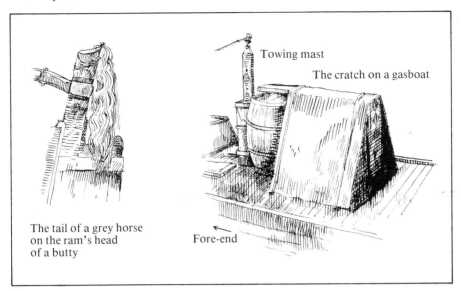

Towing mast

The cratch on a gasboat

The tail of a grey horse
on the ram's head
of a butty

Fore-end

'cratch'. This resembled a covered-in part at the front end of cargo space on ordinary narrow boats, but faced in the opposite direction. With other narrow boats a feed barrel and often bales of hay were carried in the fore-cabin or rope locker in the bows of the craft.

Horse- or mule-drawn narrow boats continued to work over shorter canals, especially in the Midlands, for some time after the Second World War, with at least four horse-drawn craft on the Worcester and Birmingham line until the 1950s, although the once-familiar towing donkeys had disappeared 30 years earlier. It is interesting to note, in this connection, that the site of former stables on the Worcester Canal at Gas Street, Birmingham, has now been converted into a smart night club, patronised by enthusiasts for motor sport, known as 'The Opposite Lock'. This may be reached along the towing path and, shortly after its opening, the blare of saxophones and popping of champagne corks were interrupted by a solitary owner-boater hammering at the door and claiming overnight stabling for his tired horse. Temporary arrangements were made in a lean-to shed at the back of the building and both man and horse were treated to the best the house could offer at short notice.

In the Black Country and on the Birmingham Canals, many narrow boats, also known as 'Joey Boats' or day boats, continued to be hauled by horses until the early 1970s. The original traffic was mainly coal or coke, using special 'coal boats', double-ended and with only a small shelter in place of a full-sized stern cabin, also with the minimum vertical features. In later years horse boats were limited to those dealing with factory waste and domestic rubbish, taken in so-called 'rubbish boats' (some owned by Birmingham Corporation) to remote sites for dumping. A single sturdy horse might be needed to haul two boats in all traffic throughout the waterways network. Two horses were less frequently worked in tandem on a pair of boats, while on rare occasions a mule worked in tandem with a horse, the smaller animal leading the way.* On the Oxford

* In coaching, with a four-in-hand team, the wheelers were often slightly larger than the leaders.

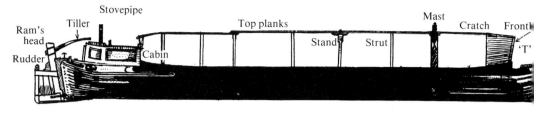

A horse-boat or butty

Canal, according to photographic evidence, there was at least one case of a pony paired with a donkey. Although empty boats were sometimes towed in trains of two or three by a single horse, especially in the Black Country, this was not often done as it tended to strain and damage the woodwork through boats bumping into each other.

The average narrow boat—as used for long distance work—carried between 25 and 31 tons of cargo, although craft using the Severn Navigation—with square bilges—carried up to 40 tons. Massive 'Ampton Boats' (Wolverhampton Boats) on a stretch of lock-free navigation between Wolverhampton and Cannock were 80 ft in length and carried between 45 and 50 tons of coal from Cannock Chase pits, although upwards of 46 tons was rare.

It is generally considered that a narrow boat fully loaded, drawn by a single horse, travelled at upwards of 2 miles per hour. An empty boat could travel a mile an hour faster, while two loaded boats pulled by a single horse (usually of the shire type) travelled at 1½ miles per hour. Distances travelled each day varied but could be upwards of 30 miles, although more often between 20 and 26 miles. Stables were situated at roughly two hourly intervals and were always on or very near the towing path. The period of work could be from dawn to dusk, especially in the early days, before the Frist World War, and sometimes well beyond this time.

On some canals there were night shifts and night boats for which extra dues were charged, especially lock tolls. Railway-owned canals eventually eliminated night work, under pressure from their staff and employees, the latter threatening strike action. Yet the demand of the railway unions that canal boaters should work the same hours as railwaymen employed by the same operating companies, gradually undermined what remained of the economic viability of narrow waterways. Earlier in the century a 16- or 17-hour day was by no means unusual for boaters or hired crews.

Fly boats ran fast services in relays, night and day, on many of the main line canals, the horses changed at various intervals, although some boats travelled upwards of 10 miles at a stretch and 20 miles was not unknown. With shorter distances between changes, horses tended to work at a much faster pace, sometimes at a trot. The crews worked in shifts, as on steam boats, two men resting in the stern cabin while one steered and the other took charge of the horse. On some lines, however, it was two men on and one man off. These services were mainly for perishable goods, worked between the London or Mersey Docks and industrial towns of the Midlands.

When a single horse pulled two boats on a narrow canal it would draw the first boat through the lock pounds while the second boat was bowhauled by a member of the family or crew. At lock flights with several pounds together, rising in a staircase effect, spare horses were later used for assisting non-powered boats or butties of a working pair in much the same way. On the Shropshire Union Canal a crewman was often sent ahead with a spare horse, to assist boats through the Audlem Flight. He frequently led or drove the horse at a smart trot, while riding a pedal cycle—on which he also hoped to return.

Tub-boats

On the tub-boat canals of Shropshire, including the Shrewsbury, Coalport and Donnington Wood Canals, a single horse would haul a train of box-like tubs, mainly used in handling coal or iron-ore for local forges and foundries. One horse would haul about 10 tubs while a pair of horses in tandem would pull 20 tubs, each tub being 19 ft 9 in long and 6 ft 2 in wide, with an average weight of 5 tons on a maximum draught of 2 in. There was a tendency for the towing animals to draw their train into the bank and, to prevent them running aground or piling-up, a man walked alongside fending them off with a shaft or bargepole. Some locks on the Shropshire tub-boat navigations were up to 81 ft in length but only 6 ft 4 in wide, allowing four tubs through at the same time, while shorter locks took three tubs each. In some places inclined planes were used at changes of level, as a substitute for lock pounds. Other horse-hauled craft to work over the Shropshire tub-boat canals were 70 ft by 6 ft 2 in wide, drawing 12½ in empty and loading to 17½ tons.

There were also tub-boat canals in South Wales and the West of England, using both men and women as bowhauliers. Perhaps the best known of these was the Bude Canal in Cornwall, where individual tub-boats had fixed wheels on either side of their hulls for ascending and descending the numerous inclined

Tub-boats on the Torrington Canal, Devon, c 1825.

Above *Loading tub-boats, Denby Colliery, Derby Canal.* **Below** *Tub-boats and horse, Shrewsbury Canal.*

planes. Bude tub-boats loaded up to 4 tons each (an example has been preserved at the Exeter Maritime Museum) and were different from the Shropshire boats in having the first craft of each train with a pointed rather than a square-ended bow.

The pointed, rather than the square, boat, preceeding a square-ended craft, was also recorded in an early engraving of the Torrington Canal (North Devon) and seems characteristic of tub-boat haulage in the West Country. The passage of each craft or train appears to have been much swifter than that of the Shropshire tub-boats, as they were drawn by much livelier horses, at least compared with the slow-moving heavyweights depicted in photographs of the West Midland navigations of this area. A system of tub-boats was first used on Parnall's Canal in Cornwall, in connection with local mines, during the first half of the 18th century. These were fairly small boats, drawn in trains by a single horse.

Container craft

It is interesting to note that container systems of transport, often regarded as modern innovations, had their origin during the latter part of the 18th century. The early 'starvationers' or cigar-shaped narrow boats used in the underground (colliery) canals of the Duke of Bridgewater, were examples of this type, their inner ribs adapted to serve as compartments into which boxes of hewn coal could be lifted near the seam face. When arriving at Worsley Basin on the surface level (via inclined planes) the loads were transferred to other craft, the starvationers then returned with empty boxes. Many horse-hauled container barges, mainly used for coal and later coke, worked in large numbers over the Bridgewater Canal until the early 1950s.

On certain lines of navigation there were also cart boats, containing laden carts of the two-wheeled variety, the shafts of each vehicle fitted neatly under the tailboard of the cart in front, to save space. Experiments in this connection were first made on the Forth and Clyde Canal in Scotland. A cart boat, drawn by a single horse, was often loaded with up to six market carts or tumbrils per boat, although forward cargo space might be shared with cattle, sheep and other livestock. Farm animals were taken to market in this manner, the sheep penned by hurdles, the pigs under nets and the cattle tethered down the centre of the craft. With large numbers of animals perhaps only two carts (or three at the most) would be carried inboard, confined to one end of the boat. When cattle and farm produce were carried the cart boats were often known as market boats.

In mining and industrial areas there were tramroad wagon-boats, also drawn by a single horse apiece. The primitive wagons (sometimes spelt waggons) or calderons arrived at the wharfside after a short journey from the pithead over a plate or wagonway. At this point the wagons were lifted into the hold or body of the craft, each boat taking up to six wagons but sometimes less. The lifting agent at the wharf would be manual crane-power. It is significant that, while teams of four or more horses were needed to bring wagons to the canalside or basin, they could be drawn through the water with greater ease and economy by a single horse. This system had many variations in both England and Scotland, lasting until the early part of the present century. It is claimed that it was invented by Benjamin Outram (1746-1805), the Derbyshire-born engineer and iron-master. Plateways leading from mine or quarry to wharf and staithe may

The Penderyn Tramway, Aberdare Canal.

well have been the ancestors of the main line railway systems, frequently owned by the canal companies—especially in South Wales—and becoming so numerous and complex that they eventually covered as much ground as the canals they served.

Perhaps the best known of the English container systems was operated by the Denby Colliery near Derby, off-loading at Little Eaton Wharf on the Derby Canal. The tramway and canal were both constructed under an Act of 1793, to serve local collieries, and remained in active service until 1908. The tubs, wagons or containers were supported on four wheels each that were flangeless, fitting outside rather than under the bodywork, although the track itself was flanged or of 'L' section. A team of four heavy horses of the shire type pulled runs of eight wagons each. Within each wagon would be boxes containing between 33 and 37½ cwts of coal, lifted directly into the boat on the wharf. The landward part of the system was known as the Little Eaton Gangway, being four miles in length, of single track but with passing loops. The wagons were 2 tons (capacity) each.

Part II
Passenger Boats

Horse or mule hauled passenger boats, also known as packet boats, were first used on the Bridgewater Canal during the 1760s. There had been a number of such boats on rivers, inlets and estuaries of Britain long before this period, but those on the Bridgewater Canal (with the possible exception of craft on the Roman Foss Dyke) were not only the first on British still water navigations but among the first to be fitted out for the purpose and run to a regular timetable. It is said that the Duke of Bridgewater, although owning numerous private coaches and carriages, while being an accomplished horseman, greatly favoured a trip in one of his own packet boats, using them whenever possible, in preference to land transport. It may be noted that all passenger boats in those days had the right of way, in preference to those carrying goods and minerals. Other boats were expected to make room for them, both at locks and bridgeholes or on open waters, this applying to all inland navigations (the only locks on the Bridgewater Canal connected the main line with the tidal Mersey at Runcorn Docks). Packet boats of the Duke of Bridgewater had a sickle-shaped knife mounted on the bows to cut the towing or mooring lines of other craft obstructing their passage, although recent theories support an idea that such knives were decorative or symbolic—perhaps a form of trade mark.

A typical early packet boat from the Bridgewater Canal was the *Duchess-Countess,* for several years stranded at Welsh Frankton on the Ellesmere or Llangollen Canal. It ran for about 50 years between Stockton Quay, Manchester and Runcorn (as a packet boat), making a daily trip between 6 am and 7 pm. This boat, in common with several others on the same waterway, was crewed by a captain, mate, horse-boy or jockey and a stewardess or boat mistress—the latter to serve drinks and refreshments. The maximum number of passengers was 30, the inner space limited by a beam of only 6 ft. Speed was about six miles per hour, the boat drawn by two horses in tandem between stages.

Towards the end of her active career the *Duchess-Countess* suffered from railway competition and was reduced to the status of a market boat carrying cattle and farm goods in one direction, back-loading with bales of fustion (twilled cotton-cloth). Her last trip in revenue service was made in 1915, after which she was sunk—with other unwanted craft—in the Big Pool at Runcorn. After several years submerged in grimy waters she was salvaged by a group of friends and used as a holiday home, and also for cruising over the Shropshire Union Canal. This was in 1934, the craft having been treated to an extensive overhaul and refit. A few years later she became the sole property of a Mr Mackie, by whom she was used as a houseboat at semi-permanent moorings, between locks, near Welsh Frankton, her final destination. This was during the wartime period and, when she began to leak, neither time nor money could be spared for repair work. It was decided to compromise by drawing her out of the water before she sank a second time, grounding her in a field on the outskirts of the village. No longer suitable for even a weekend home, the craft was offered

A scale model of The Duchess-Countess *in the Waterways Museum.*

by Mr Mackie to the British Waterways Museum, but—by this time—deterioration was so great that she could not be moved and began rotting away. Surveyed but rejected by the then curator of the Museum she was eventually sold to a local farmer for scrap and dismantled early in 1956.

A horse-drawn passenger service worked extensively over the Manchester, Bolton and Bury Canal from 1796, its large, ungainly craft having two classes with a state cabin amidships and second class passengers in the stern portion, along with goods and parcels. The Leeds and Liverpool Canal Company ran a number of packet boats until the 1840s, from the opening of the canal, mainly between Liverpool and Wigan. There were also numerous horse packets on the Aire and Calder Navigations. Passenger services were fewer and further between in the Midlands, which may have been better served with trunk roads than the north of England.

There were, however, packet boats on the Birmingham Navigations (Birmingham to Wolverhampton line), the Derby Canal and the Cromford Canal, with pleasure trips on the Ashby Canal, Oxford Canal and the Staffordshire and Worcestershire Canal. There was a short-lived flyboat service on the Oxford Canal for passengers and parcels, but this was abandoned after complaints had been made regarding damage to the banks. A weekly market and passenger boat ran between Banbury and Oxford, discontinued in 1855 as a result of railway competition which was quicker if not cheaper. The passage or market boat of the Derby Canal plied between Swarkestone and Derby, being decked-over and having both adequate seating and a fireplace or stove for the comfort of the passengers. Fares were 6d each way, the boat leaving Swarkestone early in the morning and returning at 4 o'clock in the afternoon. It eventually ran on Fridays only, this being Market Day in Derby, but was taken out of service in 1916. In the south packet boats ran over the Kennet and Avon Canal, those starting from Bradford-on-Avon had orchestral music in addition to drinks and refreshments.

Swift moving packet boats, of light and streamlined construction, some travelling at 11 or 12 miles an hour, were known as 'Flying' or 'Fly' boats. They were not only used to convey passengers and their packages or personal luggage but also a limited amount of small (valuable) items, charged above ordinary rates. They were hauled by relays of swift horses that cantered between posts or point of exchange, some even able to change tackle on the move. There were at least two horses per boat (sometimes three or four) which were varied in size and strength according to the size of the craft. They were sometimes ridden by a person on each horse, but more frequently by a single postillion riding the rear horse of a pair in tandem, guiding the fore-horse by means of whip and voice. The postillion riding the rear horse could have been almost any age from a boy or youth to a middle-aged or elderly man, but was generally lean and slight, built like a modern jockey*, known as a boy whatever his age or experience. They were remarkably agile, especially when flattening themselves along the neck of the horse to avoid low bridges or the branches of trees. The fastest craft of this type were known as 'swift boats' or packets, while the slower craft were 'mixed boats', being slightly larger and having a greater proportion of luggage and parcels space compared with passenger accommodation.

* The original meaning of jockey was a horse-keeper or dealer, rather than one riding in races or concerned only with racehorses.

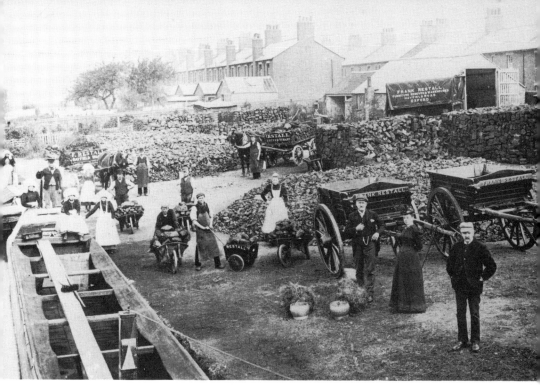

Oxford Canal Wharf, c 1895.

Swift boats had covered accommodation, almost from end-to-end, with a curved or convex roof in the centre for extra headroom. Mixed boats tended to have separate bow and stern cabins with flat roofs, there being seats for passengers and/or luggage space on the upper decks. Swift boats operating between Birmingham and Wolverhampton, shortly before the coming of the railways, were noted for their central heating by means of hot water pipes, which in those days must have been unique for a public transport system. Sitting in a warm saloon, served with drinks and hot meals—sometimes listening to the music of string bands (especially in boats on the Kennet and Avon Canal)—or playing cards or board games—must have been far more comfortable than travelling by road in even the most luxurious coach or post-chaise.

In the days when roads, apart from a few trunk routes, were roughly made and the hazards of steep gradients, mires, potholes and snow-drifts caused passengers to lighten the load or help to push, it is not surprising that horse-drawn packets remained popular until well into the railway era. Although still water canals were likely to freeze quicker and deeper than river navigations in a severe winter, even this could be controlled by the proper use of icebreakers, also horse-drawn. There was usually first, second and third class accommodation, or first and second class cabins only. The catering and the well-being of the passengers was in the hands of the captain's wife or chief stewardess, often known as the Boat Mistress.

Floods were fairly common in the low-lying eastern counties and the East Midlands. During the first half of the 19th century, packet boats were one of the few means of communication still open—for weeks on end—when roads were submerged and neither wheeled vehicles nor individual horsemen and pedestrians were able to get through. George Borrow, in the third chapter of his mainly autobiographical *Lavengro,* describes such a journey through the Fens in what he terms a treck-schuyt (Dutch for towed boat or barge), during the period of the Napoleonic Wars. He relates that, making a journey to join his father's regiment at Norman Cross, he had to embark on board 'a kind of passage-boat, crowded with people . . . drawn by horses'. The country was entirely under water, even the towing paths. 'No land was visible; the trees were growing bolt upright in the flood, whilst farmhouses and cottages were standing isolated; the horses which drew us were up to their knees in water and on coming to blind pools and greedy depths, were not infrequently swimming, in which case the boys or urchins who mounted them sometimes knelt upon the saddles and pillions.' It was further added that the horse boys (horse knockers) were well used to this kind of venture 'extricating themselves with the greatest ease from places in which Pharaoh and all his hosts would have gone to the bottom'.

Passengers on the Glasgow, Paisley and Johnstone Canal in Scotland, were drawn—during the early 19th century—in long, narrow packet boats by two horses apiece, working over four-mile stages. Each stage was completed in between 22 and 25 minutes which allowed time for people to embark and for parcels and luggage to be discharged or taken inboard. It was said that the 'boats worked over the canal at a velocity which many engineers had demonstrated but which the public had believed impossible'. The secret of swift but easy travel was for the horse or horses to make a great effort at the start of the journey, as though raising the boat through the water, which then swam near the surface on the crest of its own bow-wave, known as 'planing'.

The most advanced type of horse-drawn passenger craft was the so-called 'gig' of Scotland, based on the design of a rowing boat of the same name, being long and narrow with finely pointed bows. This was designed by William Houston of the Glasgow, Paisley and Johnstone Canal Company, each boat of this type travelling at an average speed of 10.8 miles per hour. Such craft normally had two classes for 90 passengers, with luggage compartments at each end of the hull. Passengers were seated under an awning of cotton-duck stretched over a light framework of hoops and uprights. Night boats running through the hours of darkness on the same line, were known as 'hoolets', a service commencing in 1824. Horse boys frequently sounded a warning note on a horn or trumpet, that resembled the hoot of an owl, especially late at night. Similar, almost pencil-shaped craft, were used on other waterways, in Scotland and on the Kennet and Avon Canal and the Lancaster Canal. The most successful types were iron rather than wooden craft, that seemed to slip through the water with greater ease than other vessels.

Steamers challenged horse-drawn packets during the early 1820s but, although successful on certain routes, especially when partly over estuarine or river navigations, were still only the rivals of actual horse power—on other waterways—for at least another 40 years. On the Goole Canal in Yorkshire (part of the Aire and Calder Navigations)—to name but one instance—horse boats were advertised as preferable to steamers, being more comfortable, commodious and generally safer. Regular horse-drawn packet boats ran over this section of the inland waterways, between Leeds and Goole, from 1826, so were comparatively late in their development and far from being a sentimental hang-up to which people had become attached through force of habit. They were operated in the teeth of strong opposition from the steamer captains, not by the canal company but by an independent agent, Mr J.M. Harvey, noted for his business acumen. From the early 1830s two of the largest boats in this service, renowned for their high standard of catering and cuisine, were known as *The William* and *The Adelaide,* named after the king and his popular consort (William IV and Queen Adelaide). A larger than life portrait of the King and Queen decorated the sides of each craft respectively. Both were double-hulled in catamaran-style and appear to have been constructed in yards at Wells-next-the-Sea, Norfolk, then an important barge and boat-building centre. They were withdrawn from service in 1844.

Horse-hauled boats known as 'track boats', were used on the Crinan Canal in the Highlands of Scotland as late as 1866, when they were finally replaced by the steamer *Linnet.* There were two main track boats known as *Sunbeam* and *Fair Maid of Perth,* which kept up a regular shuttle service for over 30 years, between Crinan and Ardrishaig, linking Loch Fyne (an inlet of the Firth of Clyde) with the Sound of Jura. Queen Victoria and Prince Albert made a trip through the canal in *Sunbeam* during the summer of 1847, the boat being specially refurbished for the royal party. It was drawn by four horses, one behind the other, ridden and driven by two horse boys or postillions, on the second and fourth horses respectively. The horses moved at a spanking trot, except when passing through or approaching lock pounds where they slowed to a halt, being played through by pipers in full-highland dress.

The gait and comparative quietness of horse haulage, was ideal for pleasure excursions by water and for viewing the scenery, for which it is still popular in certain parts of the country during the second half of the present century. Even from the days of their inception some owners of horse-drawn packets must have recognised this dual role and craft were fitted-out accordingly with seating on the upper decks, where this was structurally possible. Such boats were not only used as a means of getting from point A to point B but for enjoying the journey for its own sake. Some have described travel in horse boats as 'motion asleep', which speaks volumes for its soothing, almost therapeutic, effects. Perhaps the passage boats working over the Lancaster Canal between Preston and Kendal (a line now truncated by motorway crossings) were in this category, especially as it proved the main route for tourists and sightseers to reach the Lake District, without having to cross the treacherous Morecambe Sands.

According to the diary of John Fox in 1839, packets on the canal were drawn at incredible speeds, but scarcely making any wash more than a gentle swell against the bank. The horses were changed, on this line, every four miles (few relays lasting more than four miles on the early packet boat lines). In this case, however, the postillions were allowed only two minutes to change horses, returning in the opposite direction on a 60 mile stint. Yet according to Fox—speaking from the passengers viewpoint—'It was like a journey in a dream or

An aquabus, 1800

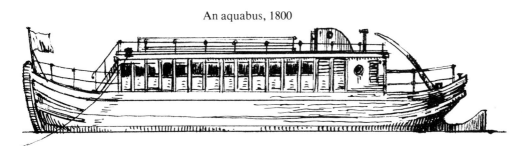

A heavy horse towing a wide boat on the Grand Union Canal, Lady Chapel's Wharf, Watford.

eastern tale, water, weather, scenery, motion—all was most beautiful'. Communication between steersman and postillion, on the Lancaster boats, was either by horn or whistle.

Other horse-drawn packets, some known as 'aquabuses', worked on short hauls over the Paddington and Regent's Canals in London, providing both useful transport and relaxation in an urban setting, especially during the first half of the 19th century. A comparatively long-distance service of this type ran via the Paddington Arm or Canal and Grand Junction Canal to a terminal basin at Uxbridge, still known as the Packet Dock Basin, about 25 miles.

Irish Boats

Ireland formerly had a magnificent network of inland waterways connecting numerous lakes, rivers and tidal estuaries. They proved expensive to construct, however, and were under-used, even during their early period of comparative prosperity. The two main artificial waterways, both dating from the late 18th century, were the Grand Canal of Ireland and the slightly later Royal Canal, both commencing in Dublin and—for a considerable distance—keeping almost to a parallel course. Although still used commercially until 1951, Irish waterways are now kept open for recreational purposes and pleasure boating only.

The Grand Canal has the distinction of being the first inland waterway in the British Isles to make widespread use of the internal combustion engine for its larger boats and barges, although horse-drawn craft were still being commissioned for taking turf fuel to the state-owned power stations after the Second World War. Much of the Irish commercial traffic consisted of bringing peat from the bogs of the interior to the main cities and ports, for which a special horse-drawn turf boat (peat boat) was designed. This appeared shortly after the inception of the Grand Canal and resembled the original (wooden-hulled) version of the Humber Keel, being high-sided with bluff bows. The last few of this type—used for their original purpose—were phased-out in 1920/21. Some later horse boats or barges were made from iron or steel or with metal sides and wooden bottoms—the latter similar to English composite boats on the Grand Union Canal and other waterways.

The Royal Canal was used almost exclusively for horse towing as the banks were considered fragile and unable to withstand the wash of faster moving or powered craft. Some horse boats remained on both lines until the end of traffic. The most popular of the later types were 60 ft long with a 13 ft beam, having an open hold and rounded stern, mainly appearing on the Grand Canal. These were known as emergency boats. Many were constructed from cheap local timber with a short expectation of life or service. Byetraders or haulage contractors usually hired boats from the navigation authorities. All boats were numbered rather than named.

Horse-drawn passenger boats, always known in Ireland as 'passage boats', were worked over the greater part of the Irish network from the 1790s, for at least 60 years. The starting points were canalside hotels, owned by the navigation companies, where there would be high standards of accommodation and adequate stabling. These were some of the finest transport hotels in Europe, at the time, and are still centres from which tourists may make excursions or shorter pleasure trips. The entertainment provided includes banquets in the old-world style and trips in decorated horse boats, the attendants wearing period costume of the 18th century, including cocked hats, powdered wigs and knee breeches. One of the modern centres for this type of activity is at Robertsbridge at the junction of the main line of the Grand Canal and the Barrow Branch, leading to the River Barrow Navigations.

Traditional Irish passage boats were drawn by two cantering horses apiece, at speeds between six and eight miles per hour, the horses changed at frequent intervals and seldom over-worked. The main superstructure of each craft was amidships with a raised forecastle deck above the bows. When passing through locks all passengers were ordered inside and the sliding doors were firmly closed to prevent spray or splashes from the gate and side paddles washing inboard. Much of the waiting in the saloons and routine work about the boat was done by young women or 'boat maids' under the supervision of a stewardess or Boat Mistress, usually the wife of the captain. A guard or guide, often an elder man well versed in local navigation, stood in the bows and shouted instructions to both postillions and helmsman—the latter not always able to see far ahead because of the high deck-cabins and superstructure. An exceptionally long passage boat on the Limerick Canal, known as *The Nonsuch* had hinged sections at bow and stern useful for passing through the shorter locks of this waterway.

Lumbering night boats, like night coaches on land, ran a cheaper service for poorer travellers on the Royal Canal. They were much slower and far more cramped and uncomfortable than day boats, notorious for using poor quality horses, perhaps too ill-formed and blemished to withstand the light of day and critical comment. Iron barges towed by heavy horses, but later by steam tugs, containing goods and parcels, were known as 'luggage boats'. These frequently ran a service complementary to the passage boats, which some of them outlasted.

Private or company-owned state barges

Private boats or barges on canals, sometimes known as 'state barges', bore a superficial resemblance to the state barges formerly used on the River Thames and other rivers by the nobility and high-ranking officials or dignitaries of church and state. They were owned by such men as the Duke of Bridgewater and the Earl of Ellesmere, with vested interests in the waterways, either for private pleasure excursions or to inspect canal developments in which they might have investments. Unlike the earlier state barges they were neither rowed nor sculled but drawn by cantering horses, each one of which would be ridden by a postillion wearing full state livery with jockey cap, shell-jacket (a waist-length tunic similar to a jacket worn in the Royal Horse Artillery), pipe-clayed leather breeches and top boots. This was a formal version of the same uniform worn by postillions on ordinary packet boats or riding and driving the horses of travelling carriages and post-chaises. Towing animals were usually well-bred coach and carriage horses, either Cleveland Bays or Yorkshire Coach Horses, similar types being used by the same noblemen to draw private coaches and other state or semi-state vehicles (state meaning full-dress or formal). The harness, however, was far more elaborate than would normally have been seen on the towing paths, the bridles having silver mountings in place of brass or steel, with family crests or coronets on studs of the blinkers (eye-pieces).

The state barge of the Earl of Ellesmere, heir to the Duke of Bridgewater, was used by Queen Victoria and Prince Albert during their visit to Worsley Hall in 1851—which included a trip along the Bridgewater Canal to Manchester and Salford. This was a highly elaborate craft, even by the standards of private barges, with gilt scrollwork and a proud figurehead. In later years it became an inspection boat on the Bridgewater Canal system, used by the engineers and directors. After 70 years drawn by horses, mainly in private hands, it was stripped of its finery, given a small petrol engine and used as a tripper boat on the Manchester Ship Canal and in Manchester Docks. It was sold for scrap in 1938 and although many thousands of pounds had been spent on its design, construction and upkeep, the highest bidding—for firewood—only reached five pounds.

An equivalent of the private or state barge was the Inspection or Committee Boat, owned by most canal companies or undertakings, in which the directors, committeemen or undertakers (on the board of a canal company the directors were often known as undertakers) made an annual tour of inspection over the waterways controlled by their concern. This was an excuse for much feasting, drinking and speech-making, a necessary duty developing into a grand social occasion, almost a ritual. Most craft of this type had costly interior fittings ranging from cut-glass windows and looking glasses to gilt and mahogany furniture with commodious wine bins. Although many of the inspection boats were eventually converted to steam or internal combustion engines—at least by the 1900s—*The Lady Hatherton* (named after a wife of the Chairman of the controlling company) on the Staffordshire and Worcestershire Canal, remained horse-drawn until the era of nationalisation in 1948. She is still afloat but now used as a private yacht, fitted with a replica hull. Launched from a Black Country boatyard in 1898, this was one of the last of the more elaborate company (inspection) boats or barges to be constructed. Because of the elaborate fittings she had to be kept on an even course and keel, any tipping or tilting being recorded by the ringing of a large bell amidships, for which the helmsman was held responsible.

Icebreakers

Right up to the 1950s icebreakers were frequently hauled by teams of horses—the latter hired from the railway companies or, especially in later years, from local farmers. Railway horses were often larger and far stronger on average than those used by other haulage companies or individual boaters. Until the mid-1950s railways were also the largest owners of heavy draught horses, a tradition continued by British Railways for the first eight or nine years of nationalisation. A team of horses (from a dozen to 24, depending on the thickness of the ice and the horses available) would haul the iron-sheathed 'breaker' through the ice-bound waters at the fastest speed they could muster, something between a jog-trot and a slow canter, rather like heavy cavalry on the battlefields of the Middle Ages. The thud of hoofs, cracking of whips and shattering of pack-ice—the latter thrown-up in all directions—made this a most spectacular event, perhaps a highlight of the year for local children of all ages, watching from the safety of overbridges.

Horse-drawn icebreakers were of two main types, one reinforced to break the ice by sheer weight and impact while the other was a 'rocking boat', drawn forward, which also swayed from side to side. The latter was the more effective and popular type, there being several survivors, one of which is displayed at the Black Country Museum, Dudley, West Midlands. It had a slatted deck with either centre-posts and ropes/rails or side post and hand grips (sometimes posts and ropes were adjusted by screw tension), to which the crew applied manual leverage, pushing and heaving from side to side so that the vessel rocked not only forward but sideways, the sideways motion aided by the rounded section of the hull amidships, that rolled with the slightest movement. There would be a crew of five or six on the rails or ropes, with a man at the helm and others to

An icebreaker and horse team, c 1900.

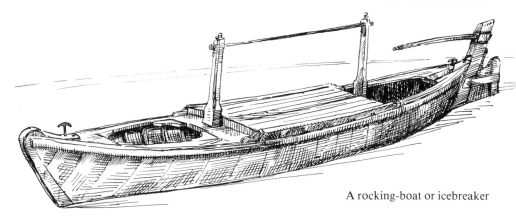

A rocking-boat or icebreaker

guide the horses. While the forward movement drove through the ice, sideways rocking increased the breakage and widened the channel.

Power boats and tugs specially fitted-up for the purpose were sometimes used as icebreakers but the majority were horse drawn, as the larger self-propelled craft tended to plane-up too far on the ice, while damage was frequently caused by the blades of the propeller striking lumps of pack-ice in which stones and other hard objects might be embedded. A few rocking boats were bowhauled and swim or square-ended, like punts, but the majority were double-ended covered with overlapping metal plates. The rudder could usually be transferred to either end to save turning.

Work in breaking the ice began as soon as the water started to freeze and was kept up at regular intervals until the thaw. Scratch crews were found from men working in the company boatyards and repair centres. During the greater part of the year the horse-drawn breaker would be kept in a side basin or backwater near the repair yard from which it operated, given an annual overhaul each Autumn. Some were kept partly submerged for greater protection of the timbers. Powered icebreakers also served a dual purpose as tunnel tugs or in drawing repair and maintenance boats to work sites. Even the most efficient icebreaker could only cope with a thickness of five or six inches. One freeze-up on the Grand Union Canal during the early 1960s was to a depth of several feet and lasted about 16 weeks, but this was exceptional.

Icebreakers of the Leeds and Liverpool Canal

These were of a unique type, much larger than other icebreakers, used only on this northern waterway. Out of season such craft were kept moored on the bank rather than the towing path side of the navigation, partly submerged but showing three or four inches of freeboard above water-level. When needed for overhaul, early in the season, they would be raised by pumping and by the use of ropes. Those used on the Yorkshire side of the Pennines were about 45 ft in length with a beam of 6 ft 6 in of 'V'-section. Side planks of the hull were vertical, extending from topline to keel—the latter made of three spliced sections (scarfed) at least 11 in square. Both bow and stern were transom-shaped or squared-off, but sloping inwards towards the keel. The fore-end of each craft was protected by a piece of bar-iron, fixed to the keel by means of an iron loop. It was shaped in the form of a shoe, projecting about a foot in advance of the prow, lifted high enough to bear down on the ice from above. The stern was slightly lower than the bows, as the rear part of the craft was ballasted by a box of heavy stones. There were three uprights in the centre of the slatted deck, with a slightly raised steering position in the stern. The masts or uprights were roped together, while the centre mast was also the towing post. Horses were guided by a man running alongside each horse.

This type of craft bore down on the ice rather than dashing into it by mere force and speed. It frequently worked—in later years—in conjunction with a powered craft (either steam or diesel), although the horse boat usually went first. When pack-ice was very thick even the horse boat planed-up, sometimes overturning on the ice and tipping its crew either on to the ice or into the freezing water.

They also served

In closing a chapter on the use of horses and mules as towing animals, it may be worth considering those of their number also used in the construction, maintenance and upkeep of canals. Thousands of horses and hundreds of mules were used for purposes of excavation and earth-moving, also hauling carts and trucks along rutted tracks, plateways or tramways. In this context it may be noted that wheelless sledge-carts were drawn over timber tracks or plankways, in the construction of Sapperton Tunnel (Thames and Severn Canal), as early as 1778. Each sledge needed two horses in the care of a single man or youth.

In the early days of construction, before the widespread use of steam engines, primitive machinery for lifting and pumping was often worked by horses or mules, harnessed to geared mechanism and forced to walk in endless circles. These were known as 'gin horses', or 'mules', wearing blindfolds to prevent them suffering attacks of giddiness. It may be noted that 'gin' was a term frequently used as an alternative for engine or even mill, but could also mean a spring trap or winding gear. Earth-moving machines, invented for use in the construction of the Gloucester and Berkeley Canal in 1793 (later the Gloucester and Sharpness Canal), were powered in this manner and may have been similar

Repair work on a vent shaft of Blisworth Tunnel, c 1890.

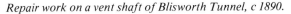

An inspection boat converted from an icebreaker.

to even earlier but less sophisticated equipment used on the Herefordshire and Gloucestershire Canal.

The Gloucester and Berkeley machinery was a labour-saving device for moving rather than digging-out soil and clay, the brain-child of Charles Brandon Trye, one of the leading shareholders of the canal company, also serving on the board of undertakers. It involved not only the raising of the skips or large containers but their latitudinal movement across the width of the canal-bed to spoil heaps some distance away, by means of an elevated ropeway. This was not a success and the system was withdrawn after a short trial period; perhaps mistrusted and misused by the workers it was intended to supplant, this being the era of the Luddite movement when supporters of a mythical 'General Ludd' were dedicated to destroy all labour-saving devices that might cause unemployment. Robert Stephenson had similar difficulties during the construction of the London to Birmingham Railway when his navvies threatened to wreck the horse-worked excavating machine he invented, unless it was dismantled and their future employment ensured.

A popular device in the later construction of railway cuttings and embankments was the so-called 'horse-run', that seems to have found favour with both management and men in all parts of the country. This was certain to have been invented for similar work on the later canals and consisted of a plankway—there being dozens of these on the same site—up the sides of a cutting, often at a steep angle. At the top of the plankway or run was a form of pulley gear suspended by an erection of upright and diagonal timbers. The barrow of a navvy at the bottom of a run was roped to the harness of a carthorse at the top. The latter moved forward at a word of command and drew both barrow and navvy up the slope, knowing exactly when to stop or turn, also keeping an even pace and straight course. The navvy merely guided the barrow up the slope, although this could be dangerous in wet and slippery weather.

Horse-drawn boats and a steam tug approaching Blisworth Tunnel.

Accidents were few and far between—seldom serious—although the odd man was known to have been killed when struck by an up-turned barrow or buried under its load. Most navvies are thought to have fallen on the runs at some time or other during their work-stints, but were usually agile enough to roll clear.

Horses were used extensively in the construction of the Caledonian Canal, both for carting spoil and overburden and as gin horses, especially to work pumps in the lock pits during their excavation. They were also used in the construction of the new Sharpness Docks on the Gloucester and Sharpness Canal, and in the excavation of the Manchester Ship Canal (which opened in 1894). The Manchester Ship Canal was the most ambitious project of its kind in Britain, during the 19th century, and the last artificial navigation to be constructed in these islands.

By the 1890s steam engines were already long-established, even common-place, including the steam-powered mechanical navvy or excavator (not having tracks but working over a length of broad gauge railway lines, although self-propelled), but many horses were still needed to draw loads of earth and builder's material beyond the railhead, working alongside clanking locomotives and steam shovels, in which was then the most highly mechanised engineering work ever attempted. On other lines horses worked into the depths of tunnels, on high embankments and across countless bridges and aqueducts—patient and usually uncomplaining—in the most arduous conditions.

The end

There was an old song among canal boaters, with more than a hint of malice, that worn-out canal horses were slaughtered and salted down for sailors (there being little love lost between deep-water seamen and the navigators of inland waterways—the latter known to sailors as 'ditch-crawlers'). Many horses appear to have died of old age or to have been worked almost to death—as in other occupations—yet once the canals had taken their toll the carcass-meat was scarcely fit for human consumption, even when disguised with great artifice in pies and cooked meats or continental-type sausages. The majority of really old and workworn horses went to kennels, zoos and menageries, also to feed the increasing numbers of cats and dogs kept as pets in suburban households. This was 'going to the dogs' in the literal and original meaning of the words, although one stage or market place removed from the towing paths.

Although at the end of its career the canal horse or mule was worth far more dead than alive—hair, hide, bones and hoofs all fetching a good price—until the moment of death it could always provide an important secondary function. Its manure was collected with loving care, on the towing path and especially from canalside stables and the middens of inn yards, and used either to grow magnificent roses in the gardens of lock keepers, or to make 'chalico'. The latter was a mixture of hot tar, cow-hair and horse manure, supplied to the boatyards as a dressing for the timbers of wooden craft. For nearly 200 years it was considered superior to any known substitute, especially during the stages of boat construction. In later years horse manure was sold by the canal companies (often under contract) to individual buyers or to farmers and market gardeners, on a well-organised commercial basis. One of the pioneers of this enterprise was the firm of William Stevens and Sons of Guildford, controlling the Wey Navigations.

Chapter 4

Acquisition and upkeep

Horses and mules for canal work could be acquired in many different ways. The haulage and canal companies owning large stables would employ a buyer or agent to act for them, making contacts with farmers, dealers and anyone having horses at their disposal. These were men of great experience who knew exactly what they needed and could tell at a glance whether or not a horse was worth buying. Those who deal in horses, especially the more shady and dubious types, have an almost oriental passion for bargaining, but the agent for a large haulage firm would make an offer beyond dispute with minimum waste of time.

Smaller men and owner-boaters might deal amongst themselves or buy horses at local markets and fairs. They would seldom be literate enough to advertise or answer advertisements in the press, although news of fairs and sales spread by word of mouth and were often discussed in taprooms of canalside inns. At one time nearly every town of any size had its street known as the 'Horse Fair' which, although a public right of way, would have broad, slightly sloping standings, below the level of the ordinary pavement, where horses, mules and donkeys would be tethered for inspection but trotted up and down the centre road (on request) to show their paces. There would be a regular sale day when those not interested in horse flesh would be well advised to keep clear of that part of the town. At one time horses were sold in the market places or cattle markets along with cows, sheep and pigs, a pattern to which a few country towns reverted—having fewer horses to sell—after the Second World War. With the great increase in the human population and the number of horses subsequently needed for commercial purposes, from the mid-19th century, it became necessary to have separate horse-marts either as covered yards or in the open.

The better class of horse, bought for a gentleman's stable, would be sold under cover, along with harness and vehicles, in what was known as a repository, this having overnight accommodation for animals brought-in from distant parts. Repository should not, however, be confused with depository, the latter being a place of storage for furniture and inanimate objects. It may be noted that special horse fairs were held at Horncastle, Stow-in-the-Wold, Barnett, Bromsgrove, Appleby and Woodbridge, with important mixed fairs for cattle and horses at Ormskirk, Rugby, Exeter, Carlisle, Lincoln, Wrexham and Falkirk. The mixed fair at Falkirk in Scotland was the largest in the British Isles and one of the most important in Europe, also being a great pleasure fair boasting three or four tenting circuses held at the same time. The main cattle and horse fairs in Ireland were Ballinasloe (at the western terminus of the Grand

Horses waiting for boats at the entrance to Braunston Tunnel.

Canal of Ireland), Dungarvan and Cahirmee (where an agent for Napoleon I, is said to have bought his master's famous charger 'Marengo'). These were held for countless generations and still attract large crowds during the second half of the 20th century.

Mention should also be made of the so-called 'Dirty Fair' held annually near Market Drayton in Shropshire, serving both the West Midlands and northern part of the Welsh Marshes. This was not as important—on a national scale—as some of the other fairs mentioned but merits a whole chapter in *Narrow Boat* by L.T.C. Rolt and was a buying point for the nearby Shropshire Union Canal (Shroppie Cut), while the Trent and Mersey Canal was not far distant.

The average canal boater could usually manage a day off if he were self-employed, leaving a spare hand or member of the family in charge for a few hours. Those with the confidence to buy for themselves would consider the costs and losses involved all part of making a deal. It is unlikely that such men would journey very far or attend the more important sales conducted by auctioneers with household names. The average number one would be more at home in the street markets of Birmingham, Coventry, Kidderminster or other centres in the Midlands, and at the more accessible country fairs such as the Dirty Fair. Here not only local horses would be encountered but a cross-section of all types and breeds, some imported in bulk from abroad, others cast from the army (branded with the letter 'C' as unfit for further military service), commercial stables or even the studs of the nobility and gentry. Rich and fashionable people sold their horses for the least fault or blemish and a lucky buyer could often find an animal which, although unwanted by its previous owner, might be offered at a bargain price, 'with four good legs and years of work in them'.

Most horses could live to between 20 and 30, although very few would be much use for serious work beyond their 20th year or several years before that age is reached. The best age for hard work is between 5 and 12, which is also the best for health and fitness. Much depends on individual treatment but, on entering double figures, a horse is considered aged and declining.

Men with a short purse, yet dependent on a horse for their way of life, were seldom squeamish or over-sentimental. Minor faults and weaknesses of a new purchase were ignored or worked out of the system, sometimes using harsh measures at which the average owner might cavil through fear of arrest or public interference. Canals were more private places than roads or even fields in which to settle disputes between horse and man, where an awkward, high-spirited creature could be flogged or starved into submission without much notice being taken.

While many boaters enjoyed a day off to make bargains in horse flesh, hinting at Romany ancestry (which although unproved may have influenced at least a few boat families), others enjoyed making deals on their own account, along the towing path. They might keep a horse for a short while, improving its appearance or disguising its faults and, by dint of pampering, produce an animal they could sell at a profit. A number of boaters were known to have made extra beer money, if not large fortunes, in this way and were for ever changing their horses to good account.

Some dealers specialised in selling horses to canal boaters and had stables or paddocks near the line of a canal where tempting offers were always on show. Other firms acted as jobbers and hired horses and mules to boaters, just as boats and other equipment were also on weekly hire or hire-purchase; a good way for a younger son without prospects to start on his own. Hiring was frequently done by the Anderton, Mersey and Weaver Navigation Companies. On the River Severn Navigations, horses could be hired from the towing path companies, sometimes with drivers, for long or short distance hauls.

The price of horses varied according to demand, size and age but £25/£30 would be considered a fair average. There was a sharp rise in prices during the First World War, followed by a slump when so many ex-army horses flooded the market after the conflict and there was an increased interest in farm mechanisation. Prices began to fall during the 1920s but were restored during the late 1930s by general inflation.

Meals

Horses needed, if they did not always get, at least three meals a day, feeding either in stables or from a nose can or bowl on the move, the motto being 'little and often'. Nose cans replaced the nosebags of the ordinary draught horse and were originally wooden bowls but were later metal cans or tins, still termed bowls by more conservative boaters until after the Second World War. In some parts, however, a feed basket was used, usually woven from withies in the style of a larger than average shopping basket. Stopping places where feed cans were replenished soon came to be recognised by experienced horses, who refused to budge from these spots until receiving attention. On the main line of the Shropshire Union Canal there were four feed stops on a daily run of 26 miles between Autherley Junction and Market Drayton.

Grazing along the sides of the towing path and in the hedgerows (on rural lines) was discouraged, and eventually forbidden by regulations, as this led to

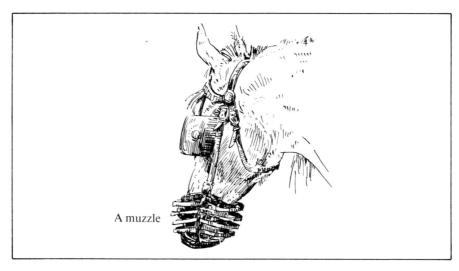

A muzzle

delays and accidents. Many animals had to wear muzzles to prevent grazing, although some wore them to curb either playful snapping or ill-tempered biting. On the Loughborough Canal and some other waterways muzzles were compulsory for all towing animals. They were regulation wear on the Worcester and Birmingham Canal from 1909.

Stables

All canal horses and mules had cause to be grateful for the widespread use of stables or shelters at night. Unlike the horses of Romany people, tinkers and some travelling showmen, they were not expected to endure 24 hours in the open which, although acceptable in good weather at certain seasons, was far from ideal between November and March, especially on the open heath. Stables were provided at intervals along the towing paths, often at a wayside inn or near a flight of locks, sometimes at the head or end of a line, or near a junction between two navigations. Such places would usually have a shop or general stores (keeping late hours), a boat-chandlers and a place of refreshment. Here a boater could moor for the night, make a few purchases, see to minor repairs and enjoy a pint of ale in the snug taproom. Yet before he could relax or attend to other matters the horse had to be stabled and given its last feed—the more thoughtful boater seeing that it had a second grooming or good rub-down. If it had been a wet day it was also advisable to dry and air the harness. The harness was usually hung on or near the stall in which the horse slept but in some of the better establishments there was a special drying room where it could be kept overnight.

Horses had to be stabled each night according to company regulations and various bylaws. Even when horses and mules were kept waiting for an hour or so they would be stabled for short periods, or (ideally) sheeted-up under special horse cloths, when standing in the open, to prevent them becoming chilled. The horse cloth was a type of sheet made of canvas, often stamped or stencilled with the name of the individual owner or firm to which the horse belonged.

There were company-owned stable blocks on or near every large wharf in canal towns, some of which also had accommodation for the horses of owner-

Above *Disused stables, Shropshire Union Canal.* **Below** *Stables near Kintilloch, Forth and Clyde Canal.* **Bottom** *Stable at Hack Green Top Lock, Shropshire Union Canal.*

An old stable floor at Hack Green, after demolition of the stables, 1977.

boaters and those passing through, not directly concerned with the business of the stable owners. The Lancaster Canal built 11 such blocks between Preston and Kendal on the main line of their waterway. While usually separate buildings, the stables were sometimes part of a larger block such as a barn, forage-store or warehouse. Fees were charged per night or portion of a day, perhaps 6d to 8d (old money) for a long stay and as little as 2d (old money) for a much shorter interval. These prices were the same in most parts of the country and comparable with those of canalside inns. It was also possible for non-company boaters to buy fodder for their horses or mules from company stables at fixed rates.

Many of the larger stables, especially those run by the canal companies or large haulage firms, would be open day and night, with a night staff to look after late arrivals and the horses of fly-boaters, working round the clock. Perhaps the least satisfactory stables for boat and barge horses were known as 'hovels', to be found on the upper reaches of the Thames Navigation, little better than open-sided sheds or shelters with turf roofs, some of which were used well into the second half of the 19th century.

Some of the finest stables along the waterways were built for Messrs (Matthew) Pickfords, the haulage contractors, who gave up their canal boats—both horse boats and steamers—during the 1850s. Although designed by the horse department of this firm, they were built by the canal companies with the aim of ensuring Pickford's valuable trade and good will, which did not seem to last, although most buildings were left in the hands of reliable tenants. The Shropshire Union Canal Company also built sound stabling of advanced design being, at one time, the largest carriers on their own line, owning 328 horses for towing purposes during the year 1905. Typical Shropshire Union buildings, at intervals along their main line (Birmingham to Liverpool Canal), were brick-

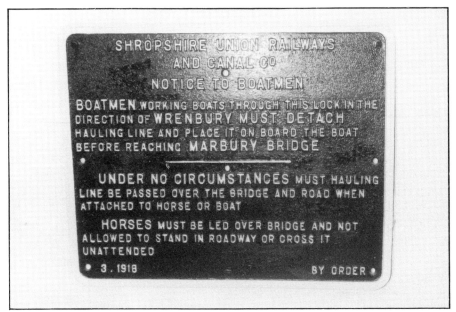

A notice to horse boaters, Waterways Museum.

built, usually with a couple roof (a roof with two opposite slopes meeting at a centre ridge), and having sufficient air space for the average number of horses using them. It is estimated that a horse of medium size used upwards of 1,000 cubic feet of air in one hour. This did not mean over-large stables but plenty of fresh air, ventilation or the proper circulation of air. Bad air led to excessive production of ammonia, a light gas that fouls the atmosphere, causing colds and coughs through irritation of both lungs and mucous membrane. Draughts, however, were to be avoided at all costs, mainly by using hopper-type windows fairly high on the walls that opened inwards and directed fresh air towards the ceiling.

The minimum height of the front wall of the stable block should have been 8 ft to the eaves but at least 8 in higher for a lean-to stable with the minimum slant of the roof. Unfortunately some of the older stables—despite their architectural charm—were often too small and overcrowded, breeding grounds for sickness and disease. Desirable roofing material would be slates or tiles, especially pantiles with improved drainage runs. Thatch, in this connection, tended to harbour insects and vermin of all kinds, while corrugated iron was too hot in summer and echoed rain and hail to such an extent that it made the horses fretful and disturbed their rest.

The Shropshire Union stables at Bunbury in Cheshire had stalls for 22 horses plus an extra loose box, which may have been used for sick or injured animals. While a loose box was generally considered better for most horses, allowing greater freedom of movement, these took up far more space than ordinary stalls in places where building land was scarce and expensive. Most loose boxes were at least 10 ft square, with a doorway or entrance of 4 ft 6 in between doorposts. The Bunbury plan seemed typical of many larger company stables throughout the country, especially those built after the 1890s. Each stall was partitioned from its neighbours, and thus known as a 'kicking stall', well drained towards the rear of the standings but not having too steep a slope—about 1 in 40 was the maximum. There would be a hayrack, manger, salt-lick and drinking trough for each stall, with room for the horse to either lie or stand. The hayrack was often very high on the wall, especially in the older stables, so that horses only reached for hay when they were hungry and not just greedy. High racks, however, had the disadvantage of allowing hayseeds to fall into the eyes of the horse, while eating, causing irritation. Modern racks were much lower and sometimes replaced by haynets. A fairly high partition of sturdy timbers, lined at the rear-ends with kicking plates, would be raised between each standing, just high enough for the horse to see its neighbour. Above five feet the partitions might have a continuation of netting or iron bars, to prevent a fretful horse from leaning across to pester those in the next stalls.

Room for the horse to lie down was essential as, although some were able to sleep or doze in a standing position, the majority liked to be recumbent for at least part of the night. Many injuries were caused in cramped, old-fashioned stables not allowing space for manoeuvre. Other horses might fall awkwardly while half-asleep and, having very little room, remain cast until help came; this, however, made them unwilling to rest properly for many nights following, as they dreaded a recurrence of their accident.

In large stables, with a couple roof, there would be a centre-gangway with

A small canalside stable for three horses

rows of stalls on each side. Smaller stables, on the lean-to plan, often had stalls on one side only, with room for two or three horses at a time, but seldom more than four. A number of the latter type seemed to fit into odd corners on the Birmingham and Black Country navigations. There were also much larger stables, in the Birmingham area, on the lean-to plan, often near a flight of locks. A few of the larger stables in all parts of the country, had two or more storeys, the upper floors reached by slatted ramps, either side or outside—the outside ones being open or covered. Covered ramps, protected from the worst of the weather, were found to be much less slippery and dangerous than open or uncovered ways. Many single-storey stables had a hay loft on the first floor, reached by outside steps and inside ladders. Corn was kept in rat-proof feed bins with heavy lids, as rats and mice not only stole unprotected food but spoilt' even more with their odour and droppings.

Company stables would employ horse-keepers and a large staff of ostlers (the head or chief-ostler, being a foreman under the horse-keeper or stable manger), grooms and stappers (men to strap or rub-down horses with a straw whisp, also engaged in harnessing and preparing a horse for work), although the stables of canalside inns—especially at the smaller inns—might leave the greater part of the work to the boaters themselves. The routine of feeding, watering and grooming began at any time after four o'clock in the morning, but sometimes even earlier, although in company stables the night shift might last two hours longer. The owner-boater stabling his horse at a canal inn or independent stables was, however, a law unto himself, often planning an early start to head the queue for a tunnel tug, or some other reasons bound up with the complexities of self-employment. Normal working hours, before the First World War, would be between 5 am and 7 pm. Before the days of electricity a start had to be made by the light of a candle or oil lamp, both dangerous to have in stables where there was so much tinder-dry fodder, and smoking was strictly forbidden by house or company rules. On winter nights and during the early mornings, water, either from the canal or trough, had to be freed of ice by tapping with an iron-bound wooden club, the latter having a slightly curved end and known as a 'hockey stick'. It was advisable to warm or at least take the chill off drinking water in these conditions, as too much chill was known to cause colic and other stomach disorders. It may be noted that a horse with colic suffered great physical pain and rolled about in such a way that it was likely to strain or rupture itself. To prevent this it had to be kept on its feet and walked up-and-down by two or more people, for hours on end.

Before the days of taps and standpipes along the canalside, water was frequently taken from the cut in a large 'boatman's bucket', but later a dipper with a short handle was used. Although not recommended for human consumption, canal water was fairly safe in most country districts, used by the boater's wife for washing clothes, cleaning up the boat and even peeling vegetables. It was frequently given to the horses, away from stables, but not in built-up areas, where the nearest canal was frequently a rubbish dump for all kinds of waste matter. Some horses were often very fussy over drinking stale or impure water, there being stretches of canal in or near industrial towns where even a horse parched with thirst would refuse to drink. Special drinking troughs were rare, apart from those in stable yards, although not unknown. In some country districts or on rural lines they appeared at the canalside, fed from a local stream or spring.

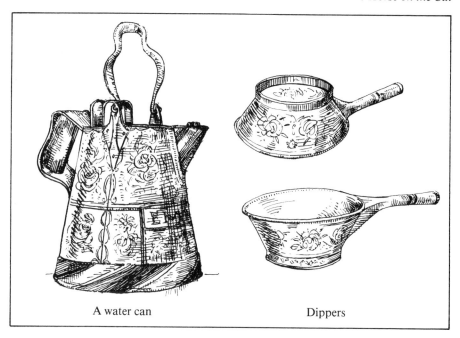

A water can   Dippers

Feed

This might depend on both the individual needs of the horse and the generosity or otherwise of its owner. In company stables feed was usually a mixture of the following, drawn in variable proportions: 8½ cwt of hay, 2½ cwt of oats and 4 cwt of chaff or grain husks. It was considered that the average heavy horse needed 8½ lbs of oats per day, plus chopped hay and bran. Hay was always left in racks or nets, at which the horse could pull, when so-inclined, at the end of the day's work. Some hay and straw were also passed through a special chopping machine with rotating blades, to make up part of the feed. This was usually hand-turned with a mangle-type wheel, known as chaff-cutters, once a feature of most barns and stable yards. Oil cake, boiled carrots and other vegetables, sometimes vegetable peelings, were offered to vary the diet and make it more interesting.

In some stables a bran mash would be offered twice a week, once mid-week and once at the weekend. Some boaters gave their horses boiled linseed to keep them in good condition, also special balls and powders (horse-balls) for the same purpose. Horses treated in this way usually had a smart, alert appearance and silken or glossy coats which were easy to groom. There were special salt-licks in many stables but some boaters preferred to sprinkle a little salt (rock salt) on the other food of the horse. According to the horsekeepers of Messrs Fellows, Morton and Clayton, Limited an (ideal) ton of mixed feed should have comprised 8½ cwt of hay, 1½ cwt of bran, 1½ cwt of peas, 2½ cwt of oats and 4 cwt of dredge (grain husks and chaff).

Oats were the necessary mainstay of the hard-working animal and those appearing lethargic or listless were often deprived of their quota. Stealing oats from the corn or feed bins was a fairly common trick in stables of all kinds, especially during the later phases of the industrial revolution, when staff were often over-worked and under-paid. In order to check on stolen oats and prevent them changing hands outside the stables, some firms (including Fellows, Morton and Clayton), introduced a percentage of coloured paper, known as confetti, into their feed bins. This was too small to cause digestive troubles or even to be noticed by the horses, but obvious enough to deter a petty thief.

Faults and vices of horses

Most of these were caused by errors of breaking, training or later mismanagement, others by fear or boredom. Boredom, often the result of isolation or under-work, was less likely to affect canal horses than those in other occupations, as they were worked too hard—as a rule—to become disinterested. It might, however, have been true of company horses kept in reserve, of which there were often several in the larger commercial stables.

One of the most annoying habits was biting that may have developed—in its early days—from the unchecked playfulness of mere nipping. It was aggravated by teasing and lack of firmness or decision on the part of the handler. The sure sign of a vicious biter (for whom the only known cure was a muzzle), would be rolling or showing the whites of the eyes and laying back the ears.

Crib-biting was often a habit of boredom, when a horse was left to itself without attention, which could seldom have happened with those engaged in canal work, except during a winter freeze-up, strike or unexpected stoppage. Crib-biting often led to wind-sucking (gulping down large quantities of air), the two habits relating to each other and inducing colic or other digestive troubles. A crib-biter would gnaw, snap and bite at any hard surface within reach—wood, leather or metal—which often caused damage to its teeth by wearing them down or snapping-off the corners. There was no permanent cure, while in some cases it would be copied by other horses sharing the same stables. Precautionary measures were to give the horse plenty of work and interest, with sufficient exercise during slack periods. It was also advisable to remove as many

Horse boats in the dock at Dudswell, Grand Union Canal.

fittings as possible from stall or box, with the exception of a haynet. In serious cases muzzling was the only answer. Crib-biting might also develop from licking the walls and woodwork of a stable, which happened through incorrect feeding or under-feeding and mineral deficiencies. In some cases it was the outward symptom of an internal parasite which disappeared when the system was cleared by purging.

Kicking was perhaps less troublesome than biting or snapping, but a great nuisance in stables, especially during grooming and harnessing. In many cases it was due to faulty grooming and the handler applying the wrong pressures to tender or ticklish parts of the body; with mares kicking was often related to the oestrus period. Heavy horses frequently kicked and stamped when troubled by itchy heels, or any other complaints suffered by those with large quantities of feather or fetlock on their lower limbs. It was also a natural tendency for horses—in the wild state—to kick in the direction of anything that annoyed or frightened them, which in stables might be scurrying rats or mice and a good reason to keep a stable cat. A bad kicker often had to be groomed with one leg held or strapped-up, but this could lead to other accidents as a horse cannot stand on three legs for very long, without danger of falling. Giving a sharp rap on the leg raised to kick accompanied by firm admonishment, was the only reliable treatment. Warning signs were a slight swaying of the body and swishing of the tail, as though brushing-off invisible insects. Inveterate kickers often wore a red warning ribbon on their tails. While a serious kick might be both painful and deadly the nearer the person was to the animal when struck, the less harmful the results. Horses kicking merely to make an interesting noise or draw attention to themselves, would sometimes have bundles of gorse or other plants with spikes and prickles hung against the sides of their stalls.

Weaving was another bad habit, in which horses swung their heads from side-to-side, sometimes rocking the body and lifting their forefeet in turn. This might be a symptom of ill health, under-nourishment or harsh treatment. It also occurs with other animals, especially when kept in small cages or pens, not large enough for reasonable exercise. Weaving was not only an ugly habit but a waste of energy, depriving the horse of its proper rest while encouraging others to follow suit, as if in sympathy. The only means of prevention was to restrain the head with side or pillar reins and to change the diet.

Treatment

In the early days canal horses may well have been under-fed, improperly fed or even over-fed, through sheer ignorance. The first men to use boat horses on the artificial waterways came from a variety of backgrounds and during the late 18th century the correct treatment or understanding of horses was far from being as widespread as it might have been even 50 years later. It is ironic that large numbers of people only came to deal knowledgeably with horses shortly before their widespread use was doomed by the internal combustion engine.

In the early days of the canal network many of those working with horses in the more conventional sphere would hold the average boater or bargee in contempt so that it was rarely the upper grades of ostler, groom or postillion who engaged in either caring for boat/barge horses or riding and driving them. Many animals underwent needless neglect and ill-treatment in consequence. Without education or training, the uninitiated might expect the horse to work like a clock or steam engine. The guiding or riding of horses along the towing paths was frequently left to young children, often in crowded conditions, when even the least perceptive child-minder or horse-fancier should have quailed. It was quoted by a visitor to the Bridgewater Canal, in the early days of passenger boats, that one of the postillions—apparently a young boy—whipped his horse 'as though sitting across a log'.

A visitor to the Birmingham Canal Navigations at a slightly later period described the horses as little better than skeletons, so under-fed that they must have learned to subsist on the scent of the water. Most of the Clayhanger novels by Arnold Bennett were written from experiences of his own boyhood and youth in the Staffordshire Potteries, where the following scene was witnessed from a canal bridge . . . 'The towing path was a morass of sticky brown mud . . . thirty yards in front of each boat an unhappy skeleton of a horse floundered its best in a quagmire. The honest endeavours of one of these animals received a frequent tonic from a bare-legged girl of seven who heartily curled the whip about its crooked large-jointed legs'. This appeared to have been on the Trent and Mersey Canal where, in later years, boaters were celebrated for the care they took of their horses.

Many cases of cruelty and neglect may be quoted, even after the passing of Acts to safeguard the welfare of animals during the 1830s, although mistrust of boaters, bargees and all travelling people—especially during the Victorian era— doubtless tended to focus more attention on detected crime involving such people than on other sections of the community. There will always be controversy as to whether company horses were treated better than others owned or hired by individuals. From 1836 the Mersey and Irwell Navigation Company appointed inspectors to walk the towing paths noting cases of ill-treatment and abuse. Owners who were detected as being at fault and failing to heed due warnings were severely punished and fined or discharged on the spot without references.

It was on the Mersey and Irwell Navigations that the famous barge horse 'Old Billy' (also a gin horse for part of his career) was employed, until the age of 62, which made him by far the oldest horse in the country (far older than most human beings during the first half of the 19th century) and at least 30 years older than any other working horses then alive. Judging from contemporary prints and paintings he was not exactly an equine beauty, even allowing for great age, and was as much a bag of bones as the towing horses described by the visitor to Birmingham during the 1780s. If ill-treatment had been his lot this surly-looking, fiddle-headed creature was certainly none the worse for the experience. By all accounts he was far from docile or sweet-tempered and gave plenty of trouble when led through the streets of Manchester in a procession to celebrate the coronation of George IV, this being two years before his death in 1822. Some people on the waterways must have cared for or taken an interest in their equine charges, responsive or otherwise, as boat horses held several records for longevity; at least three others are known to have worked well past 40 while one—owned by the Thames Navigation Company—was in full work on his 52nd birthday, but these were exceptions.

When E. Leader Williams (later Sir Edward Leader Williams), one of the most celebrated canal engineers of the Victorian era, was appointed Engineer and General Manager of the Bridgewater Canal Company he made the welfare of horses on his navigation a matter of deep personal interest. A great deal of the heavier, long distance work was soon transferred to steam packets or tugs

(known as Little Packets) during his term of office, but the remaining horses had to be treated with the greatest care and consideration. His notices to horse-keepers and drivers were displayed in all company stables and at intervals along the towing paths, with detailed instructions for the day-to-day treatment of horses and mules. They were to be worked regularly but not driven beyond their strength. On entering stables they were to be well rubbed down, until they were dry, clean and warm. If it was a cold night they were to have half water and half warm milk with a good bed shaken under them, and in no circumstances left until they were as comfortable as possible. All drivers and stable staff were to be on their guard against signs of cruelty, misuse and illness, both in their own horses and the horses of others, reporting all bruises, swellings and discharges to the office of a Mr Wall (the Company Vet) at Stockton Quay.

With effective supervision and enlightened self-interest the treatment of horses, mules and donkeys gradually improved. There were, however, exceptions, especially on the line of the Worcester and Birmingham Canal, where donkeys were still used until the early 1920s and people living near the canal complained of the way some boaters might rap and cut their animals with sticks or whips, until their hind-quarters were sore and bleeding. As late as 1931 a Joey boater on the Birmingham Navigations was reported to have flogged his horse with a length of rusty barbed wire. The ordinary whip used in these parts was terrible enough, being 30 ft long and sometimes having a small tip of lead concealed in the lash.

Horses were usually driven along the towing paths by a man or a trusted child, but seldom by a mature woman. It may be noted that the term officially used on the waterways was to drive rather than to lead or guide the horse, whatever the position of the driver. The normal position was to the right of the rear offside, with one hand on the rein leading back to the bridle and the other hand on the whip. Horses were handled in stables and taken to the farrier or vet by men, this being a masculine duty in a world with clear-cut distinctions between the work of the sexes. There were a number of exceptions but an average married woman would almost as soon drive the horse as allow her

Above left *'Old Billy'*. **Above** *A small child in charge of a boat horse, c 1925.* **Below** *A boat child about to walk the horse over a tunnel.*

husband to wash his own shirt or cook the supper. Young and attractive women, however, were sometimes photographed during the 1900s holding whips which they carried with the thong threaded through their waistband or belt. Such photographs would be taken for the family album or given to friends as keepsakes. It may be further noted that not all canal folk with whips were eager to use them on the backs of horses, as they were often carried for show, self-protection or to crack along the towing path, especially near bridgeholes, as a warning signal. Whips were often carried by the crews and owners of power boats until the mid-1930s.

Young boys and sometimes girls were frequently seen in charge of horses, by whom they were dwarfed, both on the towing paths and in streets leading to canal wharves. The boys in particular had almost a passion for riding their charges on the towing paths and along the horse paths above tunnels. Racing was a great temptation, even when riding was actually forbidden and some of the horses could muster little more than an ambling trot. On the towing paths of the Bedford Level and the East Anglian waterways, however, riding barge horses was almost commonplace and as widely accepted as driving or leading them on foot. On modern towing paths, where these still remain in fair condition, some irresponsible horsemen, women and children—sometimes from local riding schools—trot or canter their mounts without thought for the danger or damage they may be causing, to themselves, the canal banks and other towing path users. According to regulations and bylaws, however, riding horses is now only allowed in the few places where a towing path has also been designated a 'bridleway'.

On the Trent and Mersey Canal, at one period, whole sections of the towing paths would be patrolled by uniformed beadles or 'knobsticks', employed by the navigation company to keep the peace and prevent racing or riding, while acting as arbiters in disputes between boaters. These were often mounted men, the knobstick taking his nickname from a staff of office always carried on duty. Other features of their uniform, worn until the late Victorian era, was a cocked hat and long riding coat in the 18th century style. In the course of time 'knobstick' became the name not only of local security officers but for all boaters and employees on this line of canal (especially those working for the Anderton Company), also for a style of decorative art favoured by the North Staffordshire boaters.

Shows and festivals

While few canal horses were entered for ordinary horse shows, many boaters would decorate them for 'May Day' or the First of May. This was an age-old custom in town and country, thought to be of pagan origins, when even the lowliest barrowboy would spare a few coppers to decorate the browband of his pony or donkey with coloured ribbons. The knobsticks of the Trent and Mersey Canal were noted for their concern in this respect, at least during the second half of the 19th century, and took the day off to hold parades of decorated boat horses. These were also social occasions and a time of reunion with old friends and distant relations. The most outstanding of these meetings was held on May Day at Lostock Gralam, a village a few miles from Middlewich on the Trent and Mersey line. There was also a notable show and parade of boat and barge horses at Broken Cross near Nantwich. A number of local boat horse parades were

Right *Ready for the show*

Below The Horse Fair *(18th century) by Rowlandson.*

A horse fair (19th century) painted by Herring.

further held in the Potteries, during the annual Wake's Week, when factories closed and even canal boaters were given a short holiday.

There were special classes for barge horses at the (Whitsuntide) London Carthorse Parade, held in Regent's Park, with a silver cup for 'The Best Barge Horse Exhibited'. Horses were mainly entered by the towage contractors working over the London end of the Grand Union Canal system and the Regent's Canal, presented to waterways' employees acting as drivers. They appeared at the annual show on Whit-Mondays until horse towing was replaced, during the late 1950s and early 60s, by tractor-units. The chief contractors, hiring their horses—in later years—to the Inland Waterways Executive, were H.C. Barnes (Transport) Limited. Barge horses reappeared in the parade of 1975, after a break of about 15 years, although by this time the event was amalgamated with the Easter Van Horse Parade (held on Easter Mondays), now open to both commercial and private owners of heavy and light draught horses.

So-called quay flats worked into Manchester, over the River Irwell, one of these being known as the 'Old Quay Packet'. They were drawn by two horses apiece, ridden by Packet Lads or postillions. On May 1 the Old Quay Packet was dressed overall, with flags, buntings and greenery. The horses were also decorated with flowers, and large crowds gathered to witness the craft arrive at new Bailey Steps, as part of the May Day celebrations.

Doctoring

The vet was seldom called upon to tend a sick boat or barge horse, at least by owner-boaters or number-ones, unless the ailment was very serious. This also applied to the boater's themselves, most of whom would be too independent to see a doctor, unless almost too ill to be moved. Company vets were, however, employed by all the large haulage and canal navigation companies from the mid-19th century. Many boaters relied on old country and Romany recipes or prescriptions known to horsemen, on and off the cut, for generations and passed on by word of mouth. They included a popular salve made of oak bark for sores caused by chafing harness. Most sores, cuts, grazes and galls were also cured (or soothed) by a strong-smelling liniment, used by all keepers of livestock and known as 'Green Oils'. These latter were made by a respectable firm and purveyed in bottles at canalside shops, or at the chemist in the village high street, used not only on horses and mules but on the bodies of the boaters themselves—strictly for external use.

A horse or mule with a sore back was often eased by the application, twice a day, of linseed oil and turpentine well shaken together. Horses with a serious and persistent cough would be given a so-called horse-ball made from a mixture of powdered aniseed, liquorice, carraway-seed and syrup of buckthorn, up to ten nights running. A good all-round restorative, known as a 'comfortable drink' was a mixture of liquorice powder, sulphur and saffron boiled in a quart of old ale, to which a diagredium powder (acting as a strong purgative) was added when obtainable. In cases of diarrhoea the treatment was to change the diet to a thick gruel, doctoring with a mixture of powdered gentian, ginger and opium (2 drachms), given up to three times a day, over several days, until the condition improved.

Many horses in recent years suffered from colds and chills when falling into the water, through lack of maintenance on the towing paths which have been allowed to crumble away. This is considered to have been the reason for the death of Joe Skinner's last mule 'Dolly'. Carelessness and vandalism are also on the increase and a number of horses have been injured by treading on rusty cans and broken glass bottles which may have been left about by thoughtless trippers.

Horses from the Regent's Canal drinking at a Municipal Water Trough, c 1950.

Above *Shoeing a heavy horse, first removing the old shoes from the fore-feet.* **Below** *The interior of a blacksmith's shop, Bulbourne, British Waterways Depot.*

Shoeing

For company horses this would be done at a forge in or near the company stables, while other forges would be found at canalside inns. Most large stables would have not only stalls or standings but a forage-store, harness repair or saddler's shop and a smithy or shoeing forge. The latter would be much the same as the workshop of a village blacksmith, although on a larger scale, with the same array of hearth, bellows and anvil.

Most canal horses needed shoeing at least once a fortnight and seemed to wear out their 'irons' or horse-shoes even quicker than city draught or farm horses; this may have been through pressing so hard on raised or ribbed surfaces—of iron or brickwork—to gain purchase in starting a load. At the canal inns there was often a resident farrier (at least at the larger inns), also able to do other repair work on heavy materials. The Company farrier usually had two or three trained assistants or 'doormen'. Many horses that belonged to the haulage firms and canal companies or contractors were branded on one or both of their fore-hoofs with numbers and/or initials, as a means of identification. Shropshire Union Canal boaters were issued with an identity card, corresponding with the hoof numbers, which had to be shown when claiming a horse in stables or taking it to be shod.

In frosty weather, during the depths of winter, precautions often had to be taken to prevent slipping on ice. Such preparations were known to the farriers as 'roughing', which involved removing and treating the horseshoes. Calkins were formed by turning down the heels or rear parts of the shoe and, in some cases— especially with heavy horses—wedges were added to reinforce the toes. Frost nails were sometimes used in place of ordinary nails, when replacing the shoes, which were sharp, hard-headed nails intended to steady the horse on over- smooth or slippery surfaces. In later years frost or 'screw cogs' were used in place of frost nails, these having various shaped heads. They could be removed at night when the horse was taken to stables by using special keys or taps. This latter was done to prevent the horse injuring itself when scraping one leg against another. When cogs were removed the holes were filled with 'blanks' or 'blunts' to preserve the thread patterns, that might otherwise be spoilt by accumulations of grit or foreign matter. Ashes and cinders from the forge were stock piled, to scatter on the towing paths in frosty weather.

Trusts

At one period charity organisations and friendly societies, known as 'trusts', ran shelters along the towing paths (in the form of brick-built stables) where a boater could leave his horse or mule during times of personal illness or for any other reasons. These places were either free or made merely nominal charges, one of the best known and widely distributed being the 'Ingram Trust'. There was also the 'Incorporated Seamen and Boatmen's Friendly Society', which helped boaters to save for and buy their horses or boats. They were very useful when strikes, freeze-ups or repair work brought traffic to a halt and the boater found he had to fall back on savings or 'dock money'. Dock money was kept aside in case the boat needed slipping for repairs and overhaul, but also became a nickname for spare cash or savings of any kind.

Chapter 5

Work and training

Most of the canal horses were well into their prime when selected for the towing paths and at least broken to some kind of haulage work. This made the task of training easier than might otherwise have been expected, although mules and donkeys took slightly longer to acustom themselves to a routine. It was not long before towing animals responded to commands from either the boat or towing path, some experiencing a measure of independence that would have been quite new to them, having to pick their way round obstacles such as bollards, ring bolts and ground paddles, first guided but eventually left to fend for themselves while their drivers rushed ahead to secure a lock pound or mooring place. It may be noted that the bit was not always worn and sometimes hung under the chin or lower jaw.

On some canals, especially the northern part of the Staffordshire and Worcestershire line, boaters allowed their horses to 'bacca' or move unattended, while they took a rest in the stern cabin, although this was forbidden by regulations and could only be done on a quiet stretch with limited traffic and few obstacles such as locks or tunnels. The term bacca, is said to derive from tobacco and the boater enjoying a pipe during off-duty turns. The horse or mule able to bacca, or look after itself without getting its owner into trouble, was highly valued on the narrow canals; some are even said to have signalled to the steerer at the approach of other boats, by shaking their heads in a certain way or pointing with their ears. Animals were always aware of the approach of on-coming traffic long before it appeared or made warning noises.

Verbal instructions to horse, mule or donkey were often in the form of a semi-secret language shared between the animal and its driver, having variations in different parts of the country or network of inland waterways. While everyone may recognise 'whoa-there' or 'gee-up', there are also words to make a horse turn right or left, side-step, increase or slacken speed and other similar matters. Some were also taught to obey signals made by whistles, horns, trumpets or smacking whips.

The hardest part of the work, especially for the novice horse or mule, was learning to start the boat fully loaded, a task which seemed even more difficult on narrow and uneven towing paths, perhaps in a confined space near the tail of a lock. The horse or mule had to lower its head, prize its feet against the slats, sets or uneven brickwork provided in these places, and hang in the collar—but without snatching or jerking—until sufficient purchase had been gained. Once the boat began to move, however slowly, the work became easier. Many lock pounds were fitted with various forms of rollers, guides and pulley gear both on the gates and abutments or side-walls, and, by running out the towing line over and through these, greater leverage could be obtained for a standing start. Some boaters were tempted to assist their horses through a lock pound by 'flushing' or drawing water from a higher level, to create an artificial current, but this was considered a criminal waste and forbidden on most navigations. Using a towing line and pulley-block to move out of locks was known as 'blocking'. The pulley-block was fixed to the towing mast and the line (passing over its sheaves) reeled out to a pin or post at the lockside, near the head or tail of the pound. This converted ordinary purchase to a direct pull with increasing leverage until the craft was well under way. A toggle was spliced into the last ten inches or so of the towing line (known as the tack string) which, on reaching the block, cast itself off by slipping sideways from the side pin at the lockside.

When a boat ran aground or planed-up on mud or rubbish, which frequently happened on narrow canals after the Second World War, the only remedy was to lighten the load by tipping large quantities on to the bank or towing path. Although frowned upon by the authorities and other boaters this was the quickest way in which to float-off a stranded craft. This practice, however, often spoiled the level of the towing paths and later caused some horses to slip sideways into the water, especially in wet or frosty weather. Extra purchase for hauling-off was further gained by looping the towing line round the nearest mooring post, bollard or even the stump of a tree, in a crude form of blocking. Naturally enough the firmer and smoother the object used the better.

When making a broad sweep or turn through 90 degrees, bringing the boat or barge into a side arm at right angles to the main line, the driver drew a strap or short rope, attached to the fore-end stud or 'T'-stud on the bows, round a handy mooring post or upright—often provided for the purpose—thus being able to check movements of the hull that might otherwise drift into the opposite bank or plane-up (nose on) against the towing path.

Keeping a level, even pace was essential at all times but especially when drawing an empty boat, high in the water. To slacken pace in exposed areas (on rural lines) often meant the boat bumped and banged, sideways on, against the towing path, which strained the side planks and general structure. Assaulted by cross winds this was a problem for both towing animal and steerer, their combined skill aided by the driver having to fend off with shaft or pole.

The manner in which the experienced horse learned to find its way around the waterways and towing paths was little short of incredible and, while some may doubt the intelligence of equine creatures, few could fault their memories. They always recognised old haunts, even after years of absence or when some of the superficial features and details had changed, in places not always familiar to the driver. Their homing instinct was very strong, as with most domestic animals.

While some over-worked creatures on the canals had to be kept going with blows and curses, the younger and fitter animals were perhaps more difficult to stop than start, which might prove an embarrassment when a novice horse encountered other boats and horses. They soon taught themselves, however, when effort becomes not only superfluous but dangerous, as in approaching lock pounds and blind corners on towing paths. It was as if they sensed exactly when to let the rope slacken and the pace diminish to a slow halt, a trick that drivers of tractor-units—designed to replace horses, in the London area—found hard to learn, as previously mentioned.

A horse using a pulley to help start a wide boat from a lock.

When two boats met, right of way was normally given to the loaded craft, while fly boats and commercial traffic—in later years—took precedence over pleasure boats. Powered craft gave way to horse boats, just as sail, at sea or on river navigations and in estuaries, had the advantage over steam. There were often rules and regulations concerning such matters and, on waterways of industrial areas, short haul or 'Joey Boaters' were very touchy over their rights to a point of honour and were likely to start a fight on the least pretext or provocation. The driver to give way, when confronting another boat, usually brought his horse to a standstill and allowed the towing line to run slack so that approaching craft might float above it. Some boaters either detached the line or passed it overhead, but this was less frequently done than allowing it to sink, except in the West Midlands. Line raising was fairly common on the Birmingham Navigations and in the Black Country, the command made by the steerer being to 'heave it up'.

On approaching a lock pound, on most trunk routes and busy canals, there was usually an upright marking post, the person in charge of the first horse to pass such a mark having possession of the lock. Commercial traffic on most networks was divided into three groups being, in order of importance—long distance, intermediate and short haul traffic or day boaters, the latter returning home each night and regarded with a certain measure of contempt by the more professional family boaters and those working some distance from their home base.

Returning to the subject of violence, this was more serious in some areas than in others, and more likely to happen among day boaters than those on intermediate or long distance hauls. Men of the Black Country and Birmingham areas seem to have been especially quarrelsome, as were the Shropshire Union Canal boaters. They fought with belts and boathooks or shafts, smacking whips and windlass-handles (used for opening the paddles of lockgates), but most of all with their bare knuckles. Many of the Black Country boaters fancied themselves with their fists, fighting for wagers or as a means of passing the time, especially when there was a stoppage or general shortage of work. 'Caggy' Stevens, one of the last owners of commercial horse boats in this area, relates how many of the Joeys would punch a policeman on the nose for a 6d bet. Others would drag a corpse from the murkiest depths of the canal to steal its boots or the small change from trouser pockets, then throw it back to the fishes. Hardened as they were, most would risk their lives to save another from drowning, but a corpse long dead would be past help and not worth the time lost in reporting the matter.

The name 'Joey' often means a clown or foolhardy person, perhaps relating to either Joe Miller or Joseph Grimaldi, both professional stage clowns of the 18th and early 19th centuries. In this instance it may have been a title bestowed on the half-crazy characters of the Birmingham Navigations by the infinitely more responsible family or long distance boaters. While the boaters fought each other the horses might be given a rest, but this was not always the case, as the author remembers a contest on the banks of the Soar Navigation, during the early 1930s, in which not only two drivers disputed right of way but their faithful animals also went for each other with bared teeth and thrashing hoofs. The men were only persuaded to end their row to part the maddened beasts, who entered into the spirit of the fray like the troop horses and chargers of cavalrymen were said to have done during the skirmish at close-quarters.

When an obstacle on the towing path meant that a horse or mule had to be led round, the line was detached and sent forward on a wooden float, to be claimed on the further side as it drifted into bankside or towing path. This sometimes meant that the boat had to be shafted or poled for a short distance before contact with the towing line could be regained. Poling or shafting was a fairly common way in which to move craft in a shallow dock or basin, especially where there was considerable traffic and not worth risking a tangle of towing lines. It proved back-breaking work, needing the right touch and pressure to avoid being plunged into the water and perhaps crushed between boat hulls or boat and wharfside, this being a way in which many boaters and bargees were killed or injured for life. Limehouse Docks, north of the Thames, were shared by canal boats, river barges and sea-going ships, but canal craft, leaving the docks for other basins or moorings across the river or further down stream, had to be under the command of a registered Thames Waterman.

On some continental waterways, especially those in France, the horse or mule was frequently taken on board the craft it towed. It is, however, worth noting that most boats and barges in Europe were larger than their British equivalents and broader in the beam. Stables for the usual pair of towing animals, would be on the upper deck of the craft concerned, reached from the towing path or wharfside by means of a broad, slatted gangplank. On English navigations only donkeys were taken into the boat, these being small enough animals for two people to lift if they balked, jibbed or became obstinate. Donkeys were frequently carried through tunnels in this way, where there were no underground towing paths, which saved them having to be led over the top. They sometimes had a free ride when their narrow boat was towed by a steam tug, as frequently happened on the River Severn Navigations. A few boaters stabled their donkeys in empty boats for the night, to avoid paying stable fees, but this could only be done in one direction per trip.

" Git off, yer ——————————— ! "

A cartoon from Canals and Waterways Journal *entitled 'LEARNING "BOATING" '.*

Although donkeys were widely used in Ireland up to the mid-20th century, as beasts of draught and burden, there are no records of them appearing on the towing paths of the Irish waterways. In the British Isles towing by donkey seemed to have been limited to England, although a few worked a short distance into North Wales over the Welsh Section of the Shropshire Union Canal, before the First World War.

Section working

This was working boats in relays, mainly over the Staffordshire and Worcestershire Canal. Horse boats, originally heavy wooden types, but later iron or all-steel craft, were laden with coal from the Cannock pits and taken as far south as the Stewponey Wharf near Stourton, where they were handed over to a different set of men and horses for the rest of their journey. This was roughly the half-way point on the navigation, taking its name from a popular inn on the nearby Kidderminster-Wolverhampton Road, where there was extensive stabling. Crews and horses on this route worked through until Saturday lunchtime (1 o'clock) after which the horse would be stabled on the wharf, the cabins padlocked and the boaters returned home for the rest of the weekend, to be reunited with their horse and boat on Monday morning.

Although in the early days boaters on this line lived in sandstone caves—or 'rock dwellings' near Kinver, in later years they were recruited from the Tipton and Stourbridge areas of the Black Country. Some had worked in local coal boats or the pits themselves, much nearer Birmingham, but as old workings closed down they were forced to find employment further afield, especially from the 1920s. When the Kinver Light Railway or Tramway was still in operation, crossing the canal at Stewponey Bridge, they often came to work by tram. From the late 1920s they also came by motor-bus (the tramway having closed), a number of which started from the Amblecote suburb of Stourbridge, running a special service known as 'Boater's Buses' (Midland Red Omnibus Company). Canal boats on this intermediate line of navigation were similar to day boats in many respects but had slightly larger cabins.

The Staffordshire and Worcestershire Canal

Often known as the 'Stour Cut' as, for most of its route, it ran almost parallel with the River Stour. Section working, as mentioned above, was not the only feature of interest on this early line that linked the Trent and Mersey Canal with the River Severn, as Stourport-on-Severn (formerly Stourmouth) became an important leg of the 'silver cross'. In the early days it was one of the most prosperous canals in the country and carried a wide range of merchandise, transhipped to river trows or sailing barges in the special barge basin at Stourport. Because of its prosperity the line was fortunate in not being taken over by one of the main line railway companies during the second half of the 19th century. Apart from its commercial interest, Stourport was set in beautiful countryside and soon became a resort in its own right. There were both canal and river trips, although in later years navigation of the Severn was seldom more than half a mile above Stourport Bridge, which became head of commercial navigation on the river after the First World War.

The former importance of Bewdley, four miles further up-stream, soon began to diminish after a line of canal from the Black Country, locked into the Severn at the hamlet of Stourmouth, near Lower Mitton, developed from a few scattered cottages to become a thriving inland port. People from all parts of the country came to view and admire this. Although up-river trows and barges once brought all kinds of goods from Bristol and Gloucester to wharves near Bewdley Bridge (until the late 19th century), their numbers were sadly depleted over 150 years, becoming very rare by the turn of the century.

A town of importance needed good hotels and one of the oldest and most outstanding in Stourport, from the 1770s, was The Tontine with over 80 bedrooms (although most of the rooms are now flats). This still occupies an attractive site on the river bank, backing on to an area of wharves and warehouses that must have been the busiest part of the town. There was a range of extensive stables at the rear and side of the building, but many of these were demolished after the Second World War. Considerable damage was done in this area (although there is still much worth seeing) by misguided developers and unthinking local people to whom (with the slackening of trade), canals were a non-productive eyesore. They were unable to forsee the booming leisure industry of modern times—or the fascination of industrial archaeology and transport studies.

The railways and later motor transport gradually weened the bulk of commercial traffic away from the Staffordshire and Worcestershire line—during the present century—and very soon the only regular workings (mainly horse-drawn until the end), were coal boats from the Black Country and Cannock Chase. A new electricity power station opened at Stourport shortly after the First World War, this being one of the largest in the Upper Severn Valley, needing a constant supply of coal for its boiler houses and stock piles. For about 20 years there was an almost unending flow of horse-boats, during weekdays, working what was known as 'the light run'. There had been a brief and unsuccessful experiment using electric tugs, drawing their power from overhead cables—in the Kidderminster area—but this was abandoned as too costly to install and maintain. Horses were the mainstay of coal traffic, many owned or hired by the Electricity Generating Company, handled by the firm of T.S. Elements Limited. During the Second World War they were considered to be making a vital contribution to the war effort and crews were under 'essential orders' bound to their jobs as though in reserved occupations. Yet even horse boats, although less likely to damage the waterway than powered craft, still created a certain amount of erosion and silting, also damage to towing paths. Maintenance was greatly neglected throughout the 1940s and, as a result, a large number of power station boats were unable to get through (towards the end) without lightening their loads and causing further problems. By the late 1940s electricity power, railways, coalmines and most of the canals were all nationalised and, rather than invest in virtual reconstruction of the line, coal was switched to rail and road—the latter having more powerful lobbies than the canal interest. The last horse boat delivery was made shortly after the end of the war.

There was considerable traffic over the northern section of the canal, with special basins and mooring places to serve the needs of local collieries. One of the best known of these was Foster Bridge Wharf, built as late as 1927 and mainly used by horse boats until the early 1950s. In later years there was a massive rubbish tip opposite the wharf, used by the firm of Courtaulds (Wolverhampton) Limited. Waste was carried from Courtauld's plant at Dunstall, a few miles further down the line, in special horse-drawn containers. This was the last horse traffic over the northern part of the canal, in fact, almost the last over the entire line.

There were also two important wharves at Newbridge near Tettenhall, one of which was exclusive to the coal trade. The other, and perhaps earlier of the two—both dating from the early 19th century—was involved in the hire of pleasure boats and short or long distance trips in connection with school, club or works' outings. Rowing boats were also available, from the 1880s, while a special horse-drawn trip boat was held in reserve for Sunday School parties and treats, which may have been a weekly (summer) event until the First World War. Services run from this wharf were pioneers in pleasure boating, the usual itinerary being from Newbridge to Brewood and Wheaton Aston, through green and unspoilt countryside on to the Shropshire Union line, although a short distance from some of the most depressing parts of the Black Country.

Motor boats and tugs first came to the canal during the 1920s but made less impact on this line than on many others in the industrial Midlands. The average boaters seemed greatly attached to their horses and good stabling was found in a number of convenient and unexpected places. Even the smallest wayside inn would have its stable-block and barn or forage-store, other stables being at the cottages of lock keepers, of which the lock keeper would be in charge and for which duty he would receive extra money. Such stables were still evident, at the time of writing, near both Dimmingsdale and Botterham Locks. The canalside inn with the largest block of stables on the line was the 'Anchor' at Cross Green.

During the construction of the canal great use was made of both natural and artifical sandstone caves, first as temporary homes for navvies and later as semi-permanent stabling. This was a fairly common practice in North Worcestershire and South Staffordshire (the Stour Valley) with many sandstone cave dwellings, barns and stables—even cattle shelters—used within living memory. At Kinver there were not only houses excavated from sandstone cliffs but tea rooms, amusement arcades and souvenir shops, patronised by day trippers from Birmingham and the Black Country. Some of these buildings were formerly occupied by horse-boaters working on the canal. A canalside boathouse carved from solid stanstone, on the line of the canal near Stourton, was known as the 'Devil's Den' and claimed, by some local people, to be haunted.

Mules were fairly common on the upper or northern part of the Staffordshire and Worcestershire Canal, especially on the Hatherton Branch, between Wolverhampton and Cannock. Many of these, in later years, were owned by a contractor named 'Ernie' Thomas, one of the great characters of the local waterways who later owned and organised the Calf Heath Marina. Ernie began work on the Birmingham Canal Navigations as a youth, about the period of the First World War, eventually owning a fleet of several hundred day boats, mainly horse- and mule-drawn, but later using a number of tugs. He seldom had fewer than 30 mules in his stable at any given time, although a number of his boats were frequently hired-out to other concerns. As local pits began to close down for reasons of economy, or having worked out their seams, the trade contracted and few commercial boats were needed. The Calf Heath Marina, with its pleasure boating, holiday cruises and hire-craft, was a great success from the 1960s, giving Ernie a profitable second interest during what might have been his premature retirement.

Other notable characters on the canal were known as 'Glosters', having worked up the Severn from the Gloucester and Sharpness Canal and perhaps the Stroudwater Navigation or the Thames and Severn Canal. They carried both hay and pit props to mines near the upper end of the Hatherton Branch. Props came from the Forest of Dean on the West Bank of the Severn Estuary, while hay would have originated anywhere in river or canalside meadows throughout the Vale of Gloucester or the Vale of Berkeley. Back loads on return journeys were made with coal from the pits they served, the hay fed to numerous pit ponies once used in this area. On some trips, however, the Glosters were known to ballast with apples. Many of these 'West Country' boaters used pairs of donkeys to haul their craft, rather than horses or mules. Coming from the depths of the country and frequently involved with small-holdings of their own, where they may have produced at least some of their hay, these men had more the appearance of farmers than boaters. Their soft country accents and quiet ways were in striking contrast with the agressive attitudes and Black Country twang of the younger Joey Boaters. The last of the Glosters was Jacob Rice who retired in about 1930.

At Kidderminster, a carpet manufacturing town on the southern half of the canal, there was an extensive wharf owned by the Shropshire Union Canal Company, later inherited by the London, Midland and Scottish Railway Company and used as a centre for their boatage services. Stabling was for at least ten horses. There was a regular traffic in carpets and rugs between this centre and a railway wharf at Wolverhampton. From here rolled carpets were sent by rail to all parts of the country. In 'SUC' days the boats worked fly, drawn by two horses apiece, although, when taken over by the LMS, this was changed to a slower service, the boats drawn by single horses. The last through boat on the 'carpet run' was the *Saturn* which operated until 1950 from Mill Street Wharf. The last SUC boat ran from the same wharf in 1922.

Horse boats left Kidderminster during the late afternoon of each weekday, arriving in Wolverhampton early the following morning, tracking through the hours of darkness. There were numerous late workings and night shifts on the Staffordshire and Worcestershire Canal, especially over the northern end and

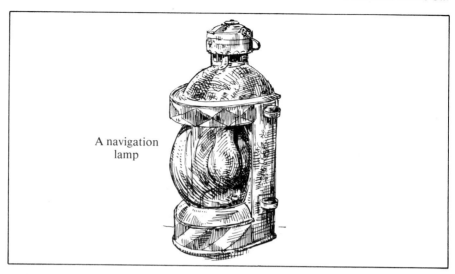

A navigation
lamp

during the Second World War, when rules may have been bent to help the war effort, most cargoes being coal and raw materials for power stations or munition factories. Iron and steel products from the numerous forges in the Stour Valley were mainly handled by Thomas Bantocks, agents for the Great Western Railway and later for the Western Region of British Railways.

On night stints motorboats were fitted with powerful electric headlamps, on or near a frontboard known as the cratch, but these were disliked by horse boaters as horses were at first dazzled by the beam of strong light, which might cause them to sidestep into the canal. The horse boats might carry a medium-sized lamp—usually an oil lamp—known as the 'masthead' or 'navigation' lamp. These were essential on a line with tunnels but were mainly associated with long distance craft. As a rule horses and mules, like many other animals, could see fairly well in the dark and the main purpose of lamps, as on horse-drawn road vehicles, was to be seen by others rather than to illuminate the path ahead. During the wartime period bridge arches were painted white, in order to show-up better at night, guiding men in charge of horses rather than the horses themselves.

The Birmingham Canal Navigations

Work over the 'BCN' was mainly in the iron and coal trade, which continued until the mid-1950s, although from the immediate post-war era many pits were either closing down, working out their seams or switching to other forms of transport and distribution. The collieries, spread out along the line of navigation, from the Cannock Extension Canal and Wyrley and Essington Branch to Halesowen and Stourbridge on the other side of the Black Country, had been there almost as long as the waterways. From the 1930s there were diesel-tugs hauling trains of four or five boats at a time, but much of the traffic continued to be horse hauled until the final pit closures. Usually it was a case of one day boat, a horse and two men (all well-known characters exchanging items of news and gossip as they passed). Typical names were Old Boffy, Old Willey, Blue Billy, Hairy Sam and Pottery Joe, friendly in their way and usually polite to strangers, but keen enough to use their fists (to dispute their rights), especially over 'First Water' in the lock pounds.

Horses with names like Nigger, Sampson, Sailor and Captain mainly fed along the towing paths as they tracked, wearing plain nose cans—usually known as 'tins'—lacking the colourful decorations of other waterways. They usually drank from the canals using the same tins, except where the water was exceptionally foul or tainted, as it might have been near certain factories and gasworks.

The average horse boat used on this line had a well-pointed bow and stern and, like most other horse-drawn craft, lacked a catwalk down the sides of the stern cabin or shelter. They were mainly on short hauls, the majority having small cabins, little more than shelters, but some being entirely open and known as 'open boats', a number of the latter used for hauling factory waste, after the coal trade declined. A few day boats were ex-long haul craft that may have seen better days and were sometimes even shortened or reduced in length. The average load was about 28 tons of coal per boat as a larger or heavier cargo would merely run aground, especially in shallow branches and side arms of the old line. Some of the shorter trips would be worked by two boats in tandem, towed by a single horse, the craft connected by means of a short line or strap. In the latter case two men would steer—one on each boat—and one man lead the horse, although sometimes the boats were 'stemmed' or close-coupled with only one steerer. Stemming, however, tended to damage the boats and spring or loosen the side planks, also battering the rudderposts.

Coal was usually loaded and unloaded at the wharfside by hand for which a man would be paid a shilling per ton. A good worker could move between 25 and 30 tons in six hours, depending on the weather and other conditions. While unloading, the boats were moored along the canalside by means of weighted chains that sank lower into the hold and drew the boat nearer in as the cargo decreased and the sides of the craft rose in the water. Many of the wharfsides and mooring places had been over-used and allowed to crumble into decrepitude through lack of maintenance.

During the Second World War whole sections of the BCN line were stanked-off at night, so that if bombs were dropped during an enemy air raid (most of these being after dark), only one part of the network would be waterless at a given time. An early morning gang toured the navigation in horse boats, removing the planks so that normal workings could begin as soon after 6 pm as possible.

The Shropshire Union Canal

Most of the craft on this navigation were owned by the SUC Company, working over its own line. Unlike other narrow boats the name of each craft would be carved rather than painted, this appearing in bold letters on either side of the stern-end. The majority were conventional family boats, but a few were lighter, smaller and swifter craft, known as 'Shroppie Flys', working as part of a relay system with precious or perishable cargoes. Able to cruise at about ten miles per hour behind cantering horses, the best known of the fly-boats on this line (known as the *Brummagem Fly*) brought cargoes of Guinness or Dublin Stout—from Liverpool Docks (via Ellesmere Port) to the centre of Birmingham. This was over a long, straight line—especially the Birmingham-

Liverpool Junction Section—frequently exposed on high embankments so that steering an empty boat, especially under stress of side winds, was always a difficult task—many tending to scrape the sides and having to be fended-off.

Horses used by the SUC boatmen were drawn from a pool owned by the company. Those used on fly boats were usually stabled apart from the ones used on normal or 'slow boat' services. The company was always keen that these horses should not be over-worked and made rest periods of up to six hours compulsory after certain runs. Some horses were obviously more willing than others and the boaters formed attachments with them. Young, keen boaters would spend their money on extra brasswork to decorate the harness, but older men would complain that the same cash was better spent 'through the nose can' or by improving the diet. Despite the identity card system boaters were not always sure of getting the same horse back if it was taken in for shoeing or vetting. For this reason some boaters with a good horse, not wishing to lose it to the pool, would pay for their own shoeing and have it done privately.

Fenland Navigations

The chief trade in this area was handled by gangs of lighters, chained together and further secured by long beams or poles, which were tightened or slackened-off—when changing direction—rather than steered in the ordinary sense. The gangs of four or five, however, had to be broken-up when entering a lock or 'pen' (East Anglian name for lock). When passing over river navigations such as the Great Ouse and its tributaries, considerable use was made of the staunch or movable dam at changes of level. This was difficult work for the towing animals, usually single horses, as, on nearing the staunch, the river narrowed and the confined current often ran strongly against them. They were assisted by kedge anchors or kedging (which was hauling up to the anchor as a form of leverage) or by the use of windlasses. When a head of water was suddenly released—on withdrawing the planks of a flush or staunch—there was a great risk of the boat being swept away, out of control, dragging men and horses with it and frequently drowning them. Many accidents of this type have been recorded on the Fenland navigations since the 17th century.

The lightermen in charge of gangs or runs were tough, hard-bitten characters, but often noted for pride in dress. Most wore a traditional costume having blue or red plush waistcoats with glass or brass buttons, narrow fustian trousers and round fur caps. They lived well on pickled beef which was kept in tubs of brine aboard the house-boat or house-lighter. When ashore they drank large quantities of ale and porter with a free allowance paid for by the owners or agents. When buying for themselves on 'tick' or account, their consumption was recorded on a board marked 'P' for pints and 'Q' for quarts, from which has been derived the saying 'mind your P's and Q's'. Such men rarely drank with their meals—mainly hunks of bread and meat—but managed to halt their gang within short walking distance of an inn, in order to enjoy a few pints after they had eaten. It was thought unwise to take drink on board the house-lighter, as this might lead to fighting and accidents.

Boys driving or riding the towing or haling horses were signed on as 'knockers', rising to 'cob-boy' or apprentice 'man 'o board'. Some skippers treated their boys with great harshness and, while many boys rode horses, others were not allowed on their backs, except to jump stiles or when the lighters were empty. Bare-footed even in winter, with snow and frost on the ground, the knockers kept up their spirits by chanting, in high-pitched voices, what are claimed to be relics of old Viking war-chants and forgotten sea-shanties.

The haling path was often obstructed by stiles or 'jumps' which the knockers took at a fairly smart trot. First they brought the horse to a halt and allowed the line to fall slack. Having looking round to make sure the line would not catch or snag they whacked the horse with a stick, kicked its flanks and took the jump in the best style possible, hoping to prevent being over-run by the barge and dragged into the water.

The Wey Navigation and Basingstoke Canal

An important centre for horse towing was over the River Wey, this being a semi-canalised navigation between Guildford and Weybridge on the River Thames, with an extension to Godalming known as the Godalming Canal. Horses remained until 1960, although haulage by tugs—using the same craft—lingered until 1969. Owners of the navigation were the family firm of Messrs William Stevens and Sons, based at Guildford. Although other boats and barges, including pleasure craft, were allowed on the Wey, after payment of tolls, commercial traffic was the monopoly of a single firm from the 1840s. Stevens also built their own craft in a special yard at Guildford, the last horse-drawn, all-wooden barge being launched in 1940. The last horse-drawn craft to ply the navigation was the *Diligent,* presented to the 'Dolphin Sailing Barge Museum Trust' by William Stevens when he retired from business and wound up the family firm. Traffic on the Wey alone exceeded 50,000 tons per annum in 1918, and for a number of years following (until 1936), after which there was a slow but steady decline.

Most Wey barges needed two horses each, working in tandem, these being of the heavy shire type. The stables were at Friary Street, Guildford, Coxes' Lock and Thames Lock. Other stables could be used on a hire basis, as required, at certain inns along the route, while stables at Thames Lock were shared with horses working over the Basingstock Canal. Towards the end of horse haulage there were six or seven horses at Friary Street, which was the main centre of operations. If extra horses were needed these were hired from a local farmer. When horses were required at Weybridge and there was no immediate return traffic, they would be taken down by road, which took 3½ hours on a good day. Working back to Guildford with a loaded barge in tow took the greater part of a single day. In later years horses were confined to the towing paths of the Wey Navigation, the barges being brought up-stream from London Docks by steam tugs.

In later years the main contractor to work over the adjacent Basingstoke Canal, from a junction with the Wey at Byfleet, was known as Harmsworth and Company, also working under contract to Stevens over the Wey Navigation. Harmsworth was in business from the 1900s until 1939, mainly concerned with an important contract to supply Working Gas Works with coal-fuel.

Concerning the Basingstoke Canal it is interesting to note that during the construction of the London-Southampton (later the London and South Western) Railway, there was an important amendment to the Act requiring the contractors to build a high wall or embankment where the railway came near the navigation, so that horses towing barges would not be frightened by the sight or sound of steam engines.

The northern waterways

On many of the northern waterways flats, lighters, keels, barges and short boats were hauled by heavy horses—either shire types or Clydesdales—frequently working in tandem, with the heavier craft. For the inland towing of keels and other estuarine craft, horses were hired for the purpose from independent stables (the horsemen in sole charge worked for the hiring firm) and were known as 'horse marines' or, less frequently, as the 'heavy brigade'. Driving or leading the horse was known as marining, even by owner-boaters. These were usually splendid animals of their kind, especially in Yorkshire, which traditionally produced some of the finest horses in Britain and perhaps the world. Mules were—at one time—greatly in evidence on the Lancashire and Cheshire side of the Pennines, especially on the Bridgewater Canal, until the second half of the 19th century.

There were many strange cargoes in the industrial north, especially over the Leeds and Liverpool Canal from the Liverpool end. These included rubbish, ashes and clinker from steamers entering the Mersey, the latter not allowed to be dumped (once over the bar), except into horse-drawn barges run alongside, based on Stanley Dock. There were also 'Muck Boats' with horse manure from commercial stables, taken to 'Muck Quays' in the country, where the contents would be collected by farmers and market gardeners. Some muck boats carried loads of dead cats and dogs for dumping, representing the thousands of annual strays and street casualties of a modern city. Loads of fruit pulp taken to jam factories saw the craft smothered in countless wasps and other insects from stem to stern. On Grand National Day many barges were cleaned up and used as grandstands for the big race, with seats at two shillings each. Special horse barges with colourful awnings, liveried servants and buffet refreshments were reserved for the directors of shipping lines.

The harnesses on the northern waterways tended to be more conservative or traditional than on the southern canals, also with a less fanciful array of horse brasses than on other waterways.

The London area

Many horse-drawn narrow boats penetrated the greater and inner London areas, working through either to Brentford or Limehouse Docks, while others terminated at the City Road or Paddington Basins. These came from out-lying parts of the Home Counties or the Midlands, especially the latter—the favourite run being London to Birmingham. On the Regent's Canal and over the Paddington Arm of the Grand Union Canal (between Paddington Basin and Bull's Bridge Junction), there was a considerable local traffic represented—until the late 1950s—by horse-drawn wide boats, lighters and similar craft. Most of these were drawn by single horses of the shire type, while tandem pairs were rare if not entirely unknown.

Large numbers of heavy draught horses were hired to the bargees or boaters by towage companies and general haulage contractors, known in the trade as 'jobbers'. These firms might also provide for the wagons and drays of road transport, especially those of coal merchants. The horses would be in the care of individual bargees or waterways employees, although returning to company stables each night, perhaps a short distance from the canals. Some were frequently seen watering at street drinking fountains and so-called cattle troughs ('cattle' was a late 18th century name for draught horses of any type), the latter

Above and below *Typical horses on the Regent's Canal.*

A heavy horse on the lower reaches of the Grand Union Canal.

once fairly common in built-up areas without access to a stream or horse-pond. Horses owned by contractors often fed from standard issue nosebags rather than from cans, bowls or nose baskets. The chains of the side traces, especially on the larger or heavier horses, might have a leather backing or lining trace on the inside, seldom using either sleeves or bobbins. Some had a short almost inflexible leather tube threaded through loops of the backband or upper part of the girth, preventing the worst effects of chafing. Along the towing paths of the Regent's Canal horses appear to have been led as much as driven, especially in later years.

Welsh canals

Horses on the canals of South Wales varied between larger or shire types and cobs, with the inevitable selection of crossbreeds, usually light rather than heavy or bulky, with the minimum fetlock. Welsh boaters seemed fond of showy brasswork, especially large face-pieces hanging below the browband, although frequently attached to an upper or crown-piece. Some of these latter were in pairs with the slightly larger face-piece at the top and the smaller face-piece below—the lower disc serving as a pendant that reached almost to the level of the noseband.

Chain traces were not always protected by bobbins or leather sleeves but there was often a wider section of the upper part of the girth, also a short leather tube, that helped to minimize galls. As with horses on the northern waterways, a plain or straight towing bar (stretcher) was used, rather than the later or bow-shaped swingle tree. Because of the many low bridges across canals, hames of the neck collars were frequently sawn-off at the tops and restricted in length.

Horses on the canals of North Wales and the Northern Marches were frequently heavy shires of a type characteristic in the farming districts of

A horse fully decked out for a special outing on the Monmouthshire Canal.

Montgomeryshire and the Shropshire border country, long renowned as a centre for horse-breeding because of the limestone basis of the pasturage. As previously mentioned, a number of donkeys were known to have operated from a wharf at Trevor on the Llangollen or Welsh section of the Shropshire Union Canal network.

On the Llangollen Canal there was a long-standing tradition of horses being ridden rather than driven on foot, which still applies to horse-drawn pleasure boats working from Llangollen Wharf. These are now mainly horses of a small 'vanner' type, ridden without saddles.

Messrs Pickfords

The first canal carrying companies were confined to northern parts of the system, including the concerns of Gilbert, Henshall and Worthington. The carrier, Matthew Pickford, already owned a large number of road wagons, eventually tendered to handle south-bound Manchester goods over the still incomplete system of inland waterways, on a national basis. His was the first company to operate a nation-wide fleet of standard boats and barges, with fly-boats for urgent traffic and perishable goods. Pickford fly-boats were soon renowned for their reliability and good time-keeping and were operated by a crew of four men per boat—sleeping in shifts or watches of two men per shift. The speed of craft in this service was an average of 3½ miles per hour, working round the clock on a 24-hour stint, interrupted only to change horses. By 1803 the firm had been established in the canal trade for about 20 years and was in a position to offer the Government (War Department) the loan of 28 horse boats in time of national emergency or invasion. There had been several cases of troops embarking for service in Ireland, taken from London to Liverpool via the inland waterways and, during the Napoleonic Wars, national strategy was

Narrow boats owned by Pickfords near the Islington Tunnel, Regent's Canal.

largely based on the use of canals and navigable rivers for defence and supply purposes. In the event of a French landing the Court and Government were to evacuate from the London area to a strongly fortified centre at Weedon on the recently opened Grand Junction Canal.

Pickfords gave up their boats as a result of a mutual agreement with the railway companies, after tendering for contracts to handle the major part of London and North Western Railway cartage and parcels distribution. Their legacy to the inland waterways was a whole range of stables and warehouses throughout the country, built to the highest standards and specifications, that soon passed to other concerns. Among other specialised cargoes, Pickfords handled considerable milk and dairy traffic, between Aylesbury and London.

Fellows, Morton and Clayton Limited

This was one of the largest and most important carrying firms in Britain to use horse haulage, on whom the mantle of Pickfords may be said to have descended. They began in a humble way as haulage contractors in the Birmingham area (Fellows) but gradually spread southwards, during the second half of the 19th century, to monopolise the trade between London and Birmingham, largely by absorbing or amalgamating with rival firms. They eventually spread to all parts of the network, their only rivals in the south being the Grand Union Canal Company (carrying on its own line), but the latter concern relied 99 per cent on the internal combustion engine from the time of its inception. The partners 'Morton' and 'Clayton' came late in the day, when the firm was first recognised as a Limited Company. Clayton also controlled a large fleet of gasboats—a line of business in which 'FMC' had no wish to be involved—based (independently) on a wharf at Oldbury, Worcestershire.

Between 1889 and 1891 there was a great danger that the firm might become bankrupt, due to the loss of towing horses caused by a prolonged epidemic of Russian Influenza, that appears to have spread over the southern half of the canal system, starting in London stables. They managed to survive but may have been scared into extending their options, becoming the owners of the largest fleet of steam-powered narrow boats in the country. These were mainly taken-over from the Grand Junction Canal Company, trading on its own line (a concern later inherited by the Grand Union Canal Company) but encountering financial difficulties through mismanagement. Regular service of steamers were operated between the City Road Basin, London, and the West Midlands, each steamer towing a haul-boat or butty. Yet because of the narrowness of the locks and other factors (the locks were widened and improved during the 1930s), the butties were dropped at Braunston and transferred to horse towing, reunited with their tugs at a point north of Hatton Locks, between Warwick and Birmingham. When Hatton Locks were rebuilt and wide enough to take two narrow boats at a time (side by side), FMC closed their stables at Braunston, saving £3,000 per annum with the added convenience of through traffic plus decreased maintenance and expenditure in the horse department. By this time the firm had mainly switched to motor boats, except on some isolated lines and in the Black Country.

Fellows, Morton and Clayton Limited kept a stable for short and intermediate workings, especially for Black Country day boats, up to the end of the Second World War when, with the nationalisation of the waterways and increasing pressure from government control, they decided to go into voluntary liquidation. As late as 1906 their horse stud was valued at £35,436, then a large investment sum, increasing by about 80 per cent over 15 years. One of the last FMC horse boats to be fully operational was used in the service of Messrs Cadbury's (chocolates and cocoa) of Bournville, Birmingham. In later years this has been displayed at the Inland Waterways Museum, Stoke Bruerne.

The main centre of operations for FMC for many years was Fazeley Street Wharf, in the centre of Birmingham, noted for its extensive repair and storage facilities, although the stables were in nearby Liverpool Street, having a blacksmith's forge, saddler's shop, sick bay for injured horses and a unique provender storage and bagging department. The FMC organisation also had extensive stabling at City Road, London, and at Preston Brook, near the junction of the Bridgewater Canal with the Trent and Mersey Canal.

West Midland fly boats

Until the period between the world wars there were regular fly boat trips between Birmingham and Ellesmere Port, at least until the mid-1920s. These were first operated by the Shropshire Union Canal Company, completing two round trips each week. They would run over the former Birmingham-Liverpool line of the SUC and the Birmingham-Wolverhampton line of the BCN, via the Wirral line, north of Chester. Each boat carried about 18 tons of general merchandise or special products, being smaller than ordinary narrow boats. They were drawn by single horses working at a fairly swift pace, with changes at various intervals, the best known being Autherley Junction, Tyrley (near Market Drayton) and Bunbury Locks, Cheshire.

A fly boat service worked over the Staffordshire and Worcestershire Canal until 1950, between Stourport, Kidderminster and Wolverhampton. It was first operated by the SUC Company, but from 1922 by the London, Midland and Scottish Railway and from 1948 by the British Inland Waterways Executive for British Railways. While the Birmingham-Ellesmere Port boats had a crew of four men the Wolverhampton boats had only three men. The boat captain on each trip was paid in advance and responsible for paying his crew and finding their food. The changing points on the Staffordshire and Worcestershire Canal were at Wolverhampton, Stewponey Wharf and Stourport. Each trip started at York Street Basin, Stourport, calling at Mill Street Wharf, Kidderminster, further up the line. The cargoes included metal products from various forges along the line, also farm produce from the Severn Valley and vinegar from Stourport. Return loads were wool and jute from Wolverhampton for the carpet mills of Kidderminster and Stourport, empty vinegar barrels for Stourport and various retail goods for Kidderminster Market (held on Thursdays and Saturdays) throughout the year. It may be noted that Kidderminster had thriving retail, wholesale and cattle markets, these being of great importance throughout the West Midlands. Goods leaving Wolverhampton before day-break were usually on market stalls later the same day. The goods agent at the Kidderminster and Stourport end of the line frequently toured the district on horseback, drumming-up trade with local farmers and merchants and booking consignments for days or weeks in advance.

Military boating

In 1917 the canal network in Britain was nationalised for the remainder of the duration and came under state control. Although playing an important part in keeping the munition factories and other vital industries in production, work on the canals was never a reserved occupation in either of the world wars. Both maintenance men and boaters were called-up for military service and although—in some cases—wives and daughters helped to keep the boats moving, the national network suffered considerably from under-manning and neglect. The best of the towing horses were also comandeered by the army to pull supply wagons on the Western Front, which led not only to a decline in the availability of horse-flesh but also inflationary prices for the remaining elderly or (comparatively) unsound horses. By the third year of the war the inland waterways system was in danger of grinding to a halt.

When the Government took over, a branch of the Royal Engineers was assigned to repairing and revitalising the waterways, operating services with horse-drawn boats and barges, usually manned by men with professional experience on the waterways in civilian life. This unit of the REs had a dual role, also training troops for service in occupied or liberated countries where much of the inland transport was water-borne. Horses used in the training sector were types rejected as unfit for overseas service, while many of the human personnel were in a low medical category, perhaps due to wounds and injuries sustained earlier in the conflict. A section of the Volunteer Reserve of the Royal Engineers was concerned with inland waterways operation until it was disbanded some years after the Second World War.

Chapter 6

Harness

The towing harness worn by canal horses and mules was usually known as tackle or tack, but sometimes as gear. A lighter version with narrower straps was worn by donkeys. Judging from early engravings and sketches, however, it appears that few donkeys wore hip or loin straps. This was a form of trace harness worn some distance from the hind quarters by beasts of draught and burden, hauling objects without either wheels or shafts (such as ploughs and harrows in farm work), or wheeled vehicles. It was suitable for drawing boats and barges along towing paths and could be adapted for timber haulage in logging and pulling trucks along rail, plate or tramways. There were no breeching straps or webs worn round the hind quarters or breeching, while the heavy cart pad or saddle (as worn by most draught horses on shafts) and the gear normally connected with shafts or poles, was absent.

Harness, for the purpose of present description, begins with the headpiece or bridle, this being a complex of medium to narrow straps of leather, adjusted to the head and face of the horse and having attachments for bit, reins, and brass ornaments. With the bridle of the average boat horse there would be vertical cheek straps on either side of the face, attached across the poll (top of the head) by a crown piece or shorter strap of almost equal width. There were two main horizontal straps, one slightly above the level of the eyes known as the browband and one some distance above the nostrils known as a noseband. Rings or loops of metal formed a connection between noseband, cheek straps and bit, which in turn connected with the reins.

Fitting to the fore-edges of the cheek straps, slightly lower than the browband, would be the 'blinkers' or 'winkers', held in place by rows of firm stitching. These were worn by most draught horses—heavy or light—especially in Britain, for at least three centuries. They were in pairs and usually near-square or rectangular, but sometimes rounded at the front, serving as leather eye-shades. They were not always worn by donkeys in draught. A metal stud in the top fore-corner of each shade connected with a lead or section of the vee-strap (v-strap) that crossed the top of the crownpiece at right angles, dividing into diagonal v-strands—left and right—just below the poll and above the forelock. The united strands of the vee-strap, behind the crownpiece, terminated in a flat loop over a throatlash or latch, slightly narrower than the other bridle straps, that buckled below the lower jaw near the junction of head and neck.

The theory behind wearing blinkers was to prevent a horse catching sight of

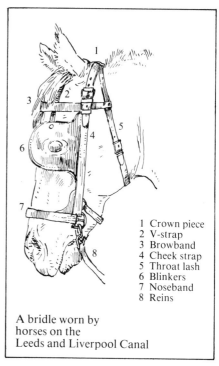

1 Crown piece
2 V-strap
3 Browband
4 Cheek strap
5 Throat lash
6 Blinkers
7 Noseband
8 Reins

A bridle worn by
horses on the
Leeds and Liverpool Canal

the object it was intended to pull, especially turning wheels, the spokes of which flashed and threw back rays of reflected light. The eyes of a horse and other members of the equine race are placed both at the sides and front of the head so that they can see quickly in several directions without too much effort or neck movement, this being a great asset in the wild state when having to rely on speed of action to escape stalking enemies. In some Continental countries blinkers were frequently ignored, especially when a horse was known to be reliable and experienced.

A small round, square or rectangular stud occupied the centre of each shade—although this was not always present—which might have the initials of the owner, a family crest or even the trade mark of the company for which the horse was working, deeply stamped or engraved to resist the effects of hard polishing. At the junction or browband and crownpiece there would be a whorl-shaped disc known as a rosette, although not always present on the bridles of some company horses, as this might be in a position for adjusting the crownpiece by strap and buckle. On other bridles the buckle was lower down and more on the side of the face.

On some canal systems horses were forced to wear muzzles, both for safety and to prevent them cropping grass along the sides of the towing path. These were either a bucket-shaped mask of firm leather with vent-holes in the lower part, or a cage of horizontal leather straps, fitting over nose, mouth and chin. They were usually carried in the stern cabin, when not worn, as a precaution. On some navigations they had to be worn at all times, when the horse or mule was not actually feeding or stabled.

The neck collar was perhaps the most important feature of draught harness,

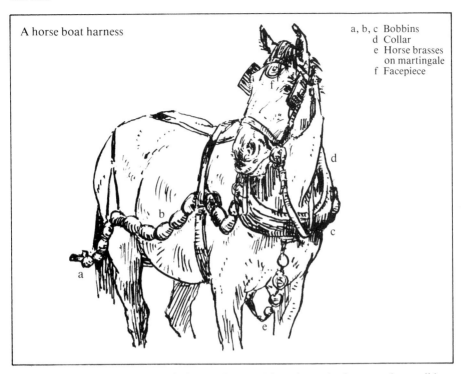

A horse boat harness

a, b, c Bobbins
d Collar
e Horse brasses
  on martingale
f Facepiece

Above far left *Bridles for draught horses.* **Below** *A boat horse in the care of a small boy.*
(A bit is not worn.)

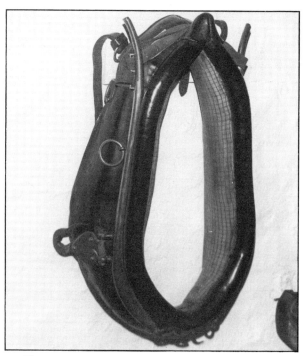

A horse collar (neck collar) in the Waterways Museum.

being the main attachment for other items of harness and an object into which the horse pushed to gain leverage or purchase over its burden. While it was commonly said that a horse pulls a cart or boat, it is really a case of pushing against the collar, which fits round the muscular junction of neck, chest and shoulders. The neck collar, although sometimes worn in Continental countries is, like blinkers, seen more frequently in Britain, especially on heavy horses, and said to suit the conformation of British draught horses (with high shoulders) better than the lighter breast harness or collar of other countries. This again is a matter of opinion but worth noting that neck collars were dropped for regular use in the British Army shortly before the First World War, although a few remained with regimental transport units and the Territorial Army throughout the period of conflict. It would be safe to say that, for heavier work with the average draught horse, a neck collar, if correctly fitted, is hard to beat. Great care should be taken in selecting and adjusting the collar, which has to be a precise fit. An awkward or ill-fitting collar might well cause terrible sores or galls, especially in wet weather. It is normally put on a horse before the bridle or other items of harness, inverted over the head, but reversed to its normal position at the base of the neck.

The construction and design of neck collars was the work of an expert craftsman, usually a specialist in this type of harness-making. The main part consists of the wale which was a leather tube stuffed with straw, reeds and/or flock, using special prods or collar sticks. This would be lined on the underside with serge, collar-cloth or basils (sheepskin). Upward curving metal bars or hames fitted into a forward groove of the collar, rising above the withers (shoulders) and terminating in decorative acorn- or knob-shapes. The tops of the hames were fairly high with a bold outward curve, following an inward curve, but on canal horses they were often (but not always), much shorter and less curved to prevent scraping arches of low bridgeholes. There was a tug hook or hame hook on either side of the collar, attached to the hames, connecting with the traces, also rein rings—the latter much nearer the top of the hames and almost level with the blinkers.

A girth or backband fitted vertically round the ribs and belly or barrel of the horse. Although there was no saddle as such, the backband was often wide enough to be mistaken for one, at least from a distance. The top half of the backband was sometimes worn without the lower part of the girth—if this were present—merely forming a connection between side traces. A false martingale or connecting strap, often loaded with brass ornaments mounted on a breastplate or piece of leather, united the lower-front part of the neck collar with the under part of the girth, passing between the forelegs. This was not always worn by donkeys, mules or lighter horses. The true martingale was associated with riding horses, providing rings and leads as an extra check for the reins—as with the so-called standing martingale.

Rearward quarter straps or hip and loin straps, of considerable length, united near the top of the croup above the pelvis of the horse, there being two such straps hanging downwards on either side of its body. On a normal draught horse harness these would support a deep, horizontal band of the breech-web—where this was worn—although the latter tended to be unfashionable for lighter horses during the second half of the 19th century. On boat horses, hip and quarter straps supported the towing bar and connected with side traces. Back and meeter straps ran down the full length of the top-back in double horizontal lines, connecting the top of the collar with the rearward harness straps and looping under the tail. There was sometimes a separate loop-strap through

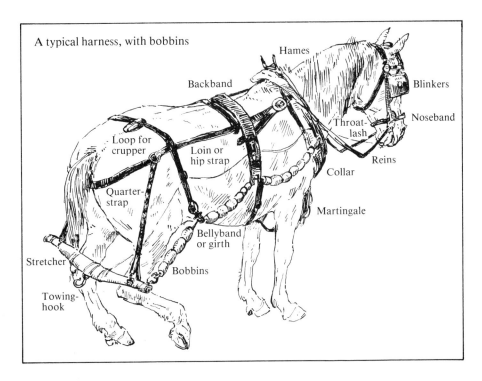

A typical harness, with bobbins

which the tail slotted, known as the crupper, although seldom worn by heavier horses and perhaps even less useful to an experienced animal than blinkers. Its function, especially when the horse drew a cart or carriage, was to prevent it getting its tail over the reins, which made driving more difficult or even dangerous through the horse gaining a measure of control. It also kept the saddle or saddle-pad from slipping forward.

Traces were parallel with the back straps but much lower down, along the sides or flanks of the body. They were attached to tug or hame hooks of the neck collar at the front and to the swingle tree or stretcher at the back. They were protected by wooden rollers that prevented them from chafing against the body or wearing thin by rubbing posts and walls along the towing path. Most traces were lengths of rope or chain, a few enclosed by leather sleeves in place of bobbins. Bobbins or rollers were in several different colours, usually reds, whites, yellows and blues. While some were rounded others were ovoid or even long and narrow.

The trace stick, track stick or bar was either a swingle tree or a stretcher, according to the part of the country and personal preference of the boater. It normally had loops and hooks or staples, for the rear-end attachment of both traces and quarter straps, adjusted by strap and buckle. The stretcher was a straight bar of painted wood, of oval or circular section, having two leads (cord or chain) at either end, attached to the towing rope. When properly adjusted it hung parallel with the towing path, just above the hocks, at right angles to the main lines of the horse . . . lifted well clear when taking the strain in draught. This type was much older than the swingle tree and continued in use on the northern waterways rather than in the south, being evident for a much longer period than other fittings. The swingle tree was a bow-shaped item with an outward or convex curve away from the hind quarters, at the apex of which would be fitted a towing hook, to take the eye of the towing line or rope. Swingle trees would be of variable sizes, sometimes adjusted by means of a central pivot. Their great advantage over the stretcher was the ease with which

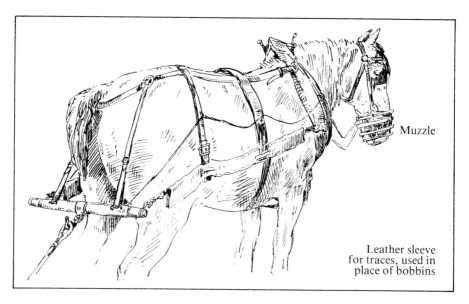

Muzzle

Leather sleeve
for traces, used in
place of bobbins

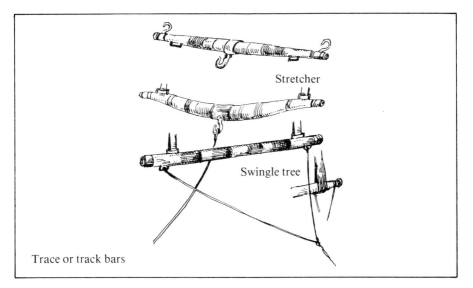

Stretcher

Swingle tree

Trace or track bars

the towing line could be cast-off or hooked-on in an emergency. The carrying firm of Fellows, Morton and Clayton Limited used a stretcher or spreader three feet long, the towing line attached to the side leads by means of a short rope-loop, grommet or gummit. Narrow reins (leather or cord) threaded back from the bridle and bit (through rein rings or terrets of the side harness).

Towing ropes or lines

These were often about 100 ft in length although the average line of a narrow boat (horse boat) was 94 ft with a weight of about 51 lb, dry. Those for river towage and barge work were usually heavier and longer with higher clearance, when attached, to avoid bankside objects such as bushes and tree stumps, while keeping as clear of the water as possible. Life of the average towing rope was six weeks at the longest. They were bought by the boaters themselves and treated with the greatest care and respect. Old ropes were often salvaged and woven into fenders and tipcats, at the boatyards.

The most popular towing lines were made of cotton as these sank easily and were thus useful when boats met or overtook each other and had to float above the line. Cotton was also strong but stretchable and elastic, which proved a great help in starting a heavy load. A novice horse making a snatch rather than a steady pull—in starting—often caused a non-cotton rope to snap. Some Black Country boaters always carried an extra length of rope for towing purposes, known as a 'tack string', although this was also a name given to the end of a rope to which a toggle was attached—used in blocking through locks, as previously mentioned. In the Black Country and on the Birmingham Navigations, hempen rather than cotton ropes were used, which may have been more traditional than other types, especially in this area.

Horse brasses

Many canal boaters gloried in their brasses or 'bright work', used as a decoration in stern cabins and on the harness of horse and mule. They were seldom seen on donkeys—at least on the towing paths—the humble canal moke

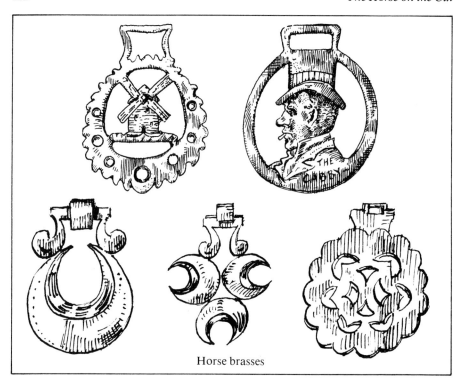

Horse brasses

rarely being considered worthy of such adornment, while the boater depending on this type of animal may have been too poor to afford unnecessary ornaments. Even in the days of steam or motor-powered craft, boaters would continue to buy and display horse brasses, hanging them on the cabin walls and in the crock cupboards. The original brasses were essentially pagan amulets, once worn by all animals of draught and burden, either to bring good luck or to ward off the evil eye. It may be noted that many of the boaters and canal dwellers were very superstitious. With canal horses brasses would be displayed on bridles and body harness in various chosen places.

The chief brasses of the bridle would be rosettes or whorls, while a round or crescent-shaped 'face-piece' lay flat on the forehead, between the eyes. Some horses even had a row of tiny bells known as latten bells (made from thin brass plate), attached to the crownpiece above the poll. On the canals these were also known as 'swingers'. This latter adornment, however, was better associated with wagon teams—the bells giving warning of their approach in winding lanes or near road junctions—being far from practical under low bridge arches, of which there were many on the narrow canals of the Midlands. Other brasses were mainly on the breastplate of the false martingale, between the forelegs, up to five in number with many regional varieties. Some were simple cross, star, shield or crescent-shapes, while others—of later design—were more intricate, representing standing or rearing horses, lions, windmills, human faces and even railway locomotives. Some were commemorative issues to record a great national event such as a Coronation, Royal Jubilee or a military victory. The most valuable, from the collector's viewpoint, are those of solid brass used by horses up to the period of the First World War. The majority now sold in curiosity and souvenir shops are cheap copies or imitations, not always made of real brass.

Apart from traditional larger brasses other parts of the body harness, especially the loin and quarter straps, were decorated with studs and inlays of polished metal in square, rounded, crescent, heart or diamond shapes. There were even squares, studs and insets of brass on the brow bands and nosebands of some bridles. Brass was expected to shine like silver, with the right amount of spit and polish, although white metal—on its own account—or chromium fittings, were far less effective.

Parts that could not be polished (on the harness and fittings) were painted or varnished. This applied to the bobbins on side traces, although in some parts of the country bobbins were replaced by a highly polished leather sleeve or cover. The ends of the swingle tree or stretcher bar would be painted with stripes or bands of bright colour, while diagonal stripes were sometimes painted on the neck collars and hames—although most boaters preferred polished metal and leather to paintwork. Even harness buckles were brass, large enough to be decorative, and round rather than square or oblong.

Nose cans

Most horses on the towing paths fed on the move, at some time or other. The exceptions were the horses of passenger or fly boats, when movement might be too swift for digestion, although stages between stables or feeding places were fairly short, by way of compensation.

The majority of boats and barges carried either one or two bowls, cans or baskets, often with a spare can or bowl on the roof of the stern cabin. The baskets, mainly used by heavier horses at the southern end of the Grand Union Canal, but also on the Wey Navigation and the Leicester Line of the Old Union Canal, were plain and undecorated, made from boiled withies. The metal cans were about 9 in deep in the centre with a diameter of about 10½ in at the base, widening outwards by 4 in at the top and bottom. They were made of tinplate, or thinly rolled iron plate dipped in molten-tin, the product of an old-fashioned tinsmith. Most external surfaces had traditional paintings, mainly based on

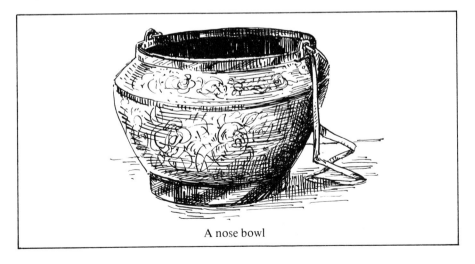

A nose bowl

A boat horse eating from a nose bowl, while a boat locks through.

patterns of roses and daisies, applied with confident, flowing brushwork. Those on the Birmingham Canal Navigations were usually left undecorated.

When not in use cans were hung from hames of the neck collar or were planted on the roof of the stern cabin, along with water can, dipper, mop and boatman's bucket. They were often displayed upside down, like the dipper, so that paintings on the base or bottom could be fully admired. When adjusted for feeding purposes, they were secured by a long strap of medium width, fitting over the top of the head, behind the ears. This latter arrangement allowed the horse to feed while tracking or waiting for a boat to pass through lock pounds. Sturdy metal construction prevented the can from being seriously damaged, although some became dented or misshapen after a few month's wear. The main disadvantage of the nose can was that if a horse fell into the cut while wearing one, this might quickly fill to the brim with water and increase the danger of drowning.

Ear protectors

In summer and hot weather many boat horses wore tasselled ear protectors, made of decorative crochetwork, usually by the boater's wife or daughters. Some, however, were sold in canalside shops or on market stalls. They fitted over the ears of the horse or mule like the fingers of a glove on a human hand, their purpose being to keep flies, midges and other creeping or stinging insects out of the ears, thus avoiding irritation. A front-piece, pelmet or valance with tasselled side strings also—in theory—kept dust and insects away from the eyes.

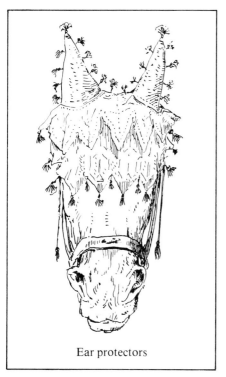

Ear protectors

Above right *A boat horse wearing ear protectors.*

While strings and tassels were brightly coloured, usually red and blue, the actual crochetwork was pure white, washed at least twice a week.

Whips

These were known as 'smacking whips', on the inland waterways. They were carried by the boaters or bargees on most of the canals, at least until the mid-1930s, almost like a badge of office. Used not only for driving horses or mules but to make warning signals by smacking or cracking (a never-to-be-forgotten sound), especially in the days before sirens and hand-horns mounted on stern cabin roofs. When not in use the thong of the whip was threaded through the waist belt and hung down the side of the leg. They were worn or carried by both men and women, especially by younger men, even the crews of steamers and early motor boats or tugs. Until the late 1920s the smart, young boater would not feel fully dressed without his smacking whip. Some were of raw hide but the majority were of plaited cord, the thong attached to the handle or stock by means of a metal loop. The length of the stock—straight and round in cross section—would be about 10 in to a foot, decorated with broad, horizontal bands of bright colours. The average length of the thong was between 10 ft and 30 ft but tended to be much longer in the north than the south.

Silk thrums

These were bought by boaters at canalside shops and sometimes on the market stalls of a canal town. They were both decorative and practical, tied to the end

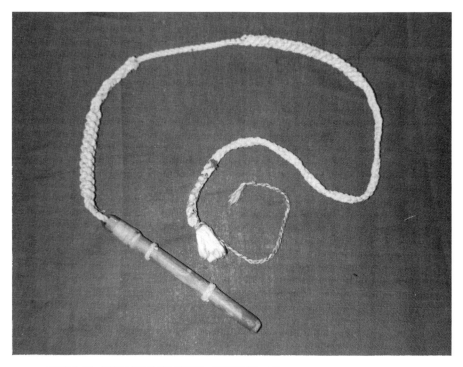

Above *A whip (smacking whip).*

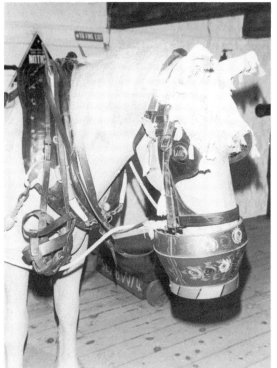

Left *A display in Waterways Museum (Stoke Bruerne) showing bridle, nose bowl, muzzle, etc.*

Above right *A boat horse with harness.*

of a whip thong to make an extra-loud cracking or smacking noise, necessary when approaching blind corners, bridgeholes or other narrow and concealed places on the navigation. There are examples on display at the Inland Waterways Museum, Stoke Bruerne.

Early forms of harness

In paintings and engravings dating back to the early 19th century, many barge and boat horses are shown with heavy chain traces, unprotected by either bobbins or leather sleeves, which do not seem to have been widely used until the middle of the century. The subsequent scars and sore places along the flanks of horses and mules must have been incredible by any standards and the use of bobbins was recommended, if not enforced, after the passing of Acts during the 1830s concerning cruelty to animals.

Many of the horses, during the early days, appear to have clumsy-looking wooden rather than leather neck collars, although roughly padded on the inner or under sides, next to the shoulders. In some cases there were only quarter straps which connected with the stretcher, without side traces. In other paintings there are neither hip nor quarter straps, the traces passing through a flat loop in the broad backband, while the stretcher hangs nearer the heels than the hocks. During the 18th century a single back strap seems to have run the entire back length, along a centre line of the spinal column, from the draught collar to a crupper-like loop, making connection with single quarter straps on either side of the croup. Barge horses of the late 18th century, on the Bridgewater Canal, wore a form of breeching web, attached to the traces near the girth, but again without hip or quarter straps. When horses towed in tandem, both animals would have stretchers, the traces from the stretcher of the first horse leading back to the traces of the rear horse.

Slow-moving and heavy barges on river navigations were towed by means of a line attached to or near the top of the mast, this latter being of considerable height, for greater clearance. A boy or youth would ride the fore-horse of a team or pair in tandem, at least during the early days. With faster moving traffic drawn by tandems—such as packets and fly boats—there would be postillions on either horse, but where there was only one rider he would be on the horse nearest the boat, which needed more control than the fore-horse or leader. In the early days, before people learned from experience, the rear horse was often unattended. When travelling at speed and perhaps ill-matched with the fore-horse, it often fell backwards into the water, having exerted most of its energy in keeping a footing on the towing path. The towing line for a swiftly moving packet boat would be placed lower down and further back than for a barge or flat and was sometimes fitted to a projecting crossbeam at the stern-end. This position assisted in planing or raising the boat on the crest of its own bow-wave.

Chapter 7

Survivals and remains

On many parts of the canal system there are still features that recall horse towing even where few horses have trodden since the Second Word War. The most obvious are the rope marks on bridges, walls and parapets caused not so much by ropes themselves but by the grit, sand and small stones collected when trailing on the towing paths. Generations of towing by horse, mule and donkey have made deep scars, often turning metal or wooden uprights, such as bollards or mooring posts, into what seem like studies in abstract sculpture. Some architectural features were protected by a steel capping or iron rollers, but even these have worn down and become distorted in due course. At the corners of buildings—along the canalside—especially near the junction of two waterways, there were often free-standing pillars or uprights to protect end walls and the lower parts (abutments) of bridgeholes.

The upright or near-vertical roller (most of them were slightly tilted) was a notable feature of the Leeds and Liverpool Canal, usually along the landward side of the towing path, especially at sudden changes of direction or where there were tight corners. Each roller was supported by a wooden baulk, like an over-sized railway sleeper. The hardwood roller was held in parallel by a ring or staple at the top and inserted into a collar or groove at the foot of its support. Its base was protected by raised paving stones. On the Lancaster Canal there were iron guard rails on the abutments of certain bridges to protect the coping stones. This is seen to full effect on the Lodge Hill towing path or side bridge, near the junction of the Glasson Branch with the main line, at Galgate.

Gates and stiles were seen along the towing paths of some waterways, but mainly on rivers. They appeared where fields came down to the margin of a waterway, making it essential to define boundaries of property. They remained longest in East Anglia and were known as 'jumps' as towing horses were forced to leap over them, when they were fixed, as explained in an earlier chapter. The regulation height was 2 ft 6 in or 2 ft 7 in but when damaged they had to be replaced and were sometimes made higher than the originals by several inches. Bargees and lightermen who suspected they were higher than average, therefore giving extra trouble to their horses, would make a point of smashing the top rails with sledge hammers carried for the purpose. The stiles remained for nearly a century and were unique to local waterways and found only in the Eastern counties. Stiles on the Arun Navigations had pivoted cross-rails with counter-weights at one end which could be depressed for a horse or man to step over them. Swing gates on the towing path of the River Soar Navigation in

A corner roller, Leeds and Liverpool Canal

Bollards and mooring posts with rope marks

Leicestershire could be pushed open by the horse poking its head forward and pressing against them with nose or forehead. Swing gates, of a self-operating type—in tubular steel—also appear on the towing path of the Weaver Navigation in Cheshire.

At various intervals along some canals, especially the Regent's Canal in London, there are so-called 'horse ramps' of stonework or concrete, leading from the towing path to below water level. These were used by horses to regain the towing path after they had accidentally fallen into the water. At one period they were also used by the boaters for washing and grooming muddy horses after a spell of bad weather, although this was frowned upon and later forbidden by the authorities as it could lead to traffic delays. The Bridgewater Canal had shallow steps or 'horse steps' serving the same purpose as ramps.

Horses could fall into the cut when brushed aside by other towing animals, or when frightened by sudden noises, especially train whistles (many canals were near both main lines and sidings), and also in wet and slippery conditions. The driver-in-charge would usually plunge after the horse or mule, attempting to free it of any gear that might entangle its limbs and cause panic. Removing the nose can would be the first priority, before this filled with water. The driver then guided the unharnessed horse to a ramp or convenient low place along the towing path side, sometimes making a temporary ramp or ledge from coping stones wrenched away from the sides of the canal, or from pieces of driftwood—of which there was always a surprising amount in or near a waterway. At this point other men and horses—with ropes as needed—might be pressed into service. The main difficulty was getting the horse to place a forefoot on dry land, after which the rest was fairly easy and straightforward.

Towing paths are now perhaps the main features to remind the observer and enthusiast of canal horses and former bank towing. These were also known as haling or hauling ways, present on certain river navigations. They were an essential feature of canal layout and construction from their inception. While river towing paths were often through fields and paddocks, especially where a farmer needed to water his livestock, they could not be fenced-off like the towing paths of canals, which latter were totally enclosed except at public wharves or where some people had access to dwellings or places of work over canal property. Riverside paths were usually much higher above the level of the waterway than those of canals and usually had numerous obstacles such as bushes, shrubs and tree stumps or saplings, the growth of which would be easier to prevent or control on an enclosed, private navigation. The importance of the hedgerow at the side of the towing path (on rural lines where it replaced walls and fences) should not be overlooked. A great deal of thought and experiment was applied to discover the most suitable growth of thick and quickset hedge for this purpose. Ideally, canalside hedges should have been cattle proof, raised on a low embankment or ridge with ditches on either side.

The average height of a canal towing path above water level was 2 ft 6 in, slightly dipped or cambered away from the edge towards the boundary hedge or wall. This cambering was to afford a better footing and balance for both men and horses, especially in wet or frosty weather. Unfortunately, due to neglect and erosion, many of the towing paths are now unusable or difficult to trace, parts

Far left and left *Rubbing posts, bridge No 62, Shropshire Union Canal.*

Cobbled sets near a lockpound, Ashton Canal.

having fallen into the canal or having disappeared under water. It was in the best interests of the canal company to keep the towing paths in good order, but this was not always done, although standards varied from one line to another. According to the survey of Mr de Salis in 1904, some towing paths, even in those days, were often: 'in winter nothing more than a slough of mire, and bounded by a hedge so overgrown as seriously to curtail the width necessary for the passage of a horse'.

Seventy years or so later the position was to become even worse, tending to limit the possible increase of horse boating for pleasure that was envisaged with the decline of commercial traffic. As originally planned the towing paths were as good or better than other well-made roads or public pathways. Some would have a foundation of large stones or rubble, well-tamped down, covered with layers of gravel or small stones known as 'raffle'. Others had a top dressing of ashes and crushed cinders, while at the approaches to bridges, locks, aqueducts and other engineering works the path would be paved with brickwork or masonry slabs to form a 'brickway', useful for greater purchase in starting a load. Slightly raised slats, bars or ridges of brickwork, sometimes reinforced with strip or bar metal, having firm, proud surfaces against which to press iron-shod heels, would help a horse or mule to gain a footing. Some canal towing paths were paved with brickwork from end to end.

There were numerous different types of bridges over inland waterways, some of which were used almost exclusively by horses. The most outstanding were the roving bridges, turn-over or change-line bridges, constructed where—for purposes of engineering or convenience of planning and land tenure—the line of

A turn-over or snake bridge

the towing path changed sides. Double towing paths were very rare and mainly appear on the new line of canal navigation—introduced by Telford—between Birmingham and Wolverhampton. A complicated type of roving bridge with three separate ramps—one crossing the canal and the others rising from the towing path—was to be found in Ireland, especially on the Ulster Canal, known as the 'ball alley bridge' because it resembled an old-fashioned skittle alley.

Ordinary accommodation bridges taking roads or pedestrian ways above canals, although sometimes built for the convenience of a farmer in cultivating his land or tending his stock, had arches of minimum span, the canal beneath them (through the 'bridgehole') reduced to little more than the width of an average narrow boat. Only one boat could scrape through at a time and it was at the approaches to such bridges that boaters signalled with their smacking whips or blew sirens.

An accommodation bridge.

Most bridges, of either accommodation or roving type, were built of stone in the north and North Midlands but of red or blue engineering bricks in the south and South Midlands. Roving bridges on the Macclesfield and Peak Forest Canals in Cheshire had high parapets and long, winding approach ramps that turned back on themselves like the coils of a serpent and were known as 'snake bridges'. Side bridges taking the towing path over the entrance to side basins or arms of the canal, often at right angles to the main line of navigation, were both steep and narrow, having ridges or footholds to assist towing animals.

On canals engineered by Brindley and his assistants there were many footbridges of the cantilever type, especially near locks and leading to lock keeper's cottages, known as 'split bridges'. These had a narrow aperture for passing the towing line without inconveniencing the horse, driver or pedestrians using the bridge. The aperture could be crossed with a normal stride. The split bridge is thought to have been invented by Brindley and is seen at its most typical on the Oxford Canal and the Staffordshire and Worcestershire Canal.

Long, narrow side bridges with fairly high parapets, usually brick-built, sometimes took towing paths over tributary streams or marshy places, perhaps near the junction of two or more waterways. They were known as 'horse bridges' and appeared in the form of an elongated side bridge but with numerous arches in place of a single arch. Several were constructed by Brindley, characterised by their small arches (too low for navigation purposes), graceful proportions and the gradual slope of the approach ramps.

At this point it is worth mentioning an iron towing path or roving bridge on the Oxford Canal, near Isis Lock, of which there were—at one time—large numbers. They were made in sections and bolted together like the modern Bailey Bridge, but were far more elegant. A characteristic feature would be the decorative side rails or balustrade, reminiscent of a regency porchway or balcony. The majority of this type were erected between 1820 and 1840.

A split bridge (with barrel-roofed cottage), Stratford Canal.

A split bridge near a lockpound

A side bridge

A snake bridge at Congleton, Macclesfield Canal.

Most of the early canal tunnels were without towing paths, including the original bore of the Harecastle Tunnel on the Trent and Mersey Canal. The second bore made by Telford, on a near-parallel line, has a shelf-like towing path on one side only protected by a rail, but this has now given way in several places and is no longer used. Where there were no underground paths, although a few canals had separate horse tunnels at a higher level, the boat would have to be disconnected from the towing animal and either legged or shafted through, often by men hired for the purpose kicking against the side walls. In a low tunnel the navigation could be sometimes 'walked' with the boater crouched on the roof of the stern cabin and kicking against the ceiling or arch of the tunnel, while in some tunnels there were side chains or other projections at which to pull. While donkeys could be taken into the boat, horses and mules had to be led over the top via specially constructed horse paths, some of which had their own taverns and places of refreshment, while others were isolated and the haunt of vagrants or drunken and irresponsible persons, by whom half-hearted attempts might be made to steal the horses.

The larger and later tunnels were frequently constructed with towing paths, at least on one side, the margin of which would have a white-painted guard rail or posts and rails to prevent the horse falling into the water. This let down to ground level at either end by means of a gradual slope to prevent the tow line snagging. Netherton Tunnel on the Birmingham Navigations, the last important tunnel to be excavated on the network of inland waterways, had double towing paths that were lit by electricity, night and day.

In some hilly districts and narrow valleys, where there were considerable changes of level and it was necessary for the towing path to change sides, this would be done by means of narrow 'horse' or 'lock' tunnels rather than roving bridges. These were at the approaches to locks and lined with masonry from which the lock pound or chamber was also constructed, having steep slopes at either end from wharf or lockside. Being expensive to construct they were few and far between and were found mainly in the Pennine region, especially near Marple Locks.

Where aqueducts were used the towing paths were often on one side only in the form of shelves, as with the towing path in Telford's line of the new Harecastle Tunnel. This had particular reference to the iron-trough crossings of Telford, with iron railings on one or both sides. On some of the earlier brickwork and masonry aqueducts of Brindley there were broad towing paths but neither guard rails nor parapets. These were omitted as an economy measure but were sometimes added at a later date.

There are still many stable-blocks intact along the towing paths, especially near basins and wharves which have been the headquarters of a canal haulage or operating company. Many are now used for a variety of purposes from storage places to workshops and club rooms. The stable-block on the wharf at Llangollen is now partly used as a waterways museum, containing many interesting relics and fine scale models to record the history and development of the canal system in Britain. Stables frequently have a unique charm and character, setting them apart from even the most attractive warehouses and other canalside buildings. Some date back to the late 18th century (when British domestic architecture was arguably at its best), although most are of Victorian design and origins. An interesting feature of many, especially the larger types with couple roofs, would be the stable clock, sometimes a small clock tower,

Below left *A horse tunnel, Cosgrove.* **Below right** *A horse tunnel, Marple flight, Macclesfield Canal.*

A canalside inn, 'The Old Wharf', Great Linform, Grand Union Canal

'The Swan',
Fradley (Staffordshire)

which would be the main timepiece for the area and important for checking work or trip schedules, especially in the days when clocks and personal watches were more expensive and less frequently used. An interesting feature of canal stables at Fradley near the junction of the Trent and Mersey Canal with the Coventry Canal, lies in the fact that they form an extension of the inn itself (The Swan) rather like a long house in rural Wales.

Wonders of the canal navigations

These are seven in number, all of which date from the days of horse towing and would have been used by horse- or mule-drawn craft. Perhaps the most outstanding, also regarded as one of the great sights or wonders of Wales, is the Pontcysyllte Aqueduct near Vron, about three and a half miles from Llangollen on the Welsh Canal or Welsh Section of the Shropshire Union Canal. This was to have been the main line of a canal linking the Midlands with either the Dee or Mersey via the mining town of Ruabon, but a link was never made and the trunk route passed north-east via the former Chester Canal. An extension of the Welsh Canal towards Ruabon formerly served stone quarries and the Plas-Kynaston Iron Works, but even this has now closed. A short distance beyond the aqueduct the only possible navigation is through a right-angled turn to Llangollen, over what was originally a feeder arm carrying water to the rest of the system (also for domestic purposes) from a junction with the River Dee at the Horse Shoe Falls, Llantysilio.

This note of explanation is needed as so many uninformed people wonder why such a remarkable engineering work appears on a mere branch canal, leading (in the commercial sense) almost nowhere. It was only some time after it was built that a decision was made to re-route the main line, although—until the coming of the railways—there was considerable traffic over the aqueduct from quarries in the upper part of the Vale of Llangollen, also coal and iron traffic to and from Plas-Kynaston.

Designed by Thomas Telford and completed in 1805, it took about ten years to build but, even by modern standards, would still be regarded as a fine achievement and Telford's masterpiece. It marches across the entrance to the Vale of Llangollen on 19 arches, the highest of which was 121 ft above the River Dee. The total length is 1,007 ft, each arch having a span of 45 ft. While the lower parts of the supporting arches are of solid masonry (dressed stone) they are hollow above 70 ft. The water way itself is carried in a cast iron trough of 12 ft width, 4 ft of which is covered by a shelf-like towing path, built over rather than beside the waterway and now fenced on one side only. There is neither guard-rail nor parapet on the navigation side and crossing the aqueduct in rough weather or on a moderately windy day is not recommended for the faint-hearted or anyone with a poor head for heights. Only a few inches of ironwork separates the boater from a sheer drop to the valley floor.

The Anderton Lift, in Cheshire, although much later in the history and development of the canals, is a further remarkable feat of engineering, combining the civil and mechanical branches of that science. It connects the lower level of the River Weaver Navigation with the Trent and Mersey Canal, about two miles from Northwich. The rise is 50 ft made in twin caissons or troughs, originally counter-balanced and worked by hydraulic power, but later converted to electrical operation so that the caissons are now independent of

Pontcysyllte aqueduct

each other. Each caisson is wide enough to take two standard narrow boats side by side. There is a sectional model of the lift at the Inland Waterways Museum, Stoke Bruerne. The prototype was designed by Sir Edward Leader Williams, Chief Engineer of the Manchester Ship Canal, also designer of the Barton Swing Aqueduct. It was opened to traffic in 1875.

The Barton Swing Aqueduct, above mentioned, takes the line of the Bridgewater Canal above the Manchester Ship Canal, both of which are now controlled by the same authority. It replaced an earlier masonry or fixed aqueduct in 1894, the original structure not being high enough for ocean-going ships that now ply between Manchester Docks and the Mersey Estuary. It is a pivoted steel trough, based on an island in the middle of the Ship Canal, normally kept in the open position to favour Bridgewater Canal traffic. The swing section is 234 ft long, 19 ft wide and 6 ft deep, sealed at both ends by rubber-lined and watertight rams. It is swung full of water to avoid delays in re-filling. The motive power is electricity.

Standedge Tunnel on the Huddersfield Narrow Canal, in the Pennine district of Yorkshire, is not only the longest but also the highest canal tunnel in Britain, above sea level. It lies between Huddersfield and the Lancashire town of Ashton-under-Lyme and once formed an important part of the canal network but is now kept open for water supply and drainage purposes only. Two tunnels of the main line railway between Manchester and Leeds traverse the same hills at a slightly higher level and are connected with the canal tunnel by means of sloping drains or adits. Standedge Tunnel is 3 miles 135 yards long, mainly unlined and cut through solid rock, but without towing paths. The interior joins together a number of extensive caverns, some of spectacular interest in their own right. It is 644 ft 9 in above the Ordnance Datum. At present the only

The Anderton boat lift

possible navigation is for inspection boats and work-flats, used to keep the tunnel in good order as a drain. The channel width is 7 ft 6 in while in parts the headroom is very limited.

Bingley Five Rise Locks on the Leeds and Liverpool Canal, at the Leeds or Yorkshire end, is 16 miles from Leeds, and assists in raising the waterway over the central part of the Pennine Range. There are five pounds or chambers, opening into each other in the form of a staircase or flight, the lower gate of one being the upper gate of the next. Navigating the flight without due care and attention may lead to sinking, drowning or even serious flooding. It is still negotiated by numerous pleasure craft, especially in summer, but those in doubt should always place themselves under the direction of the resident lock-keeper. The total rise is 60 ft.

Another feature of interest on the Leeds and Liverpool Canal is the Burnley Embankment, considered the master-work of its engineer, Robert Whitworth, a pupil and friend of James Brindley. It carries the main line of the canal for a distance of 1,256 yards above the town of Burnley, much higher than the roofs of most buildings, and proved the most expensive part of the navigation to build. Many people live in this area without fully understanding its meaning or original purpose, not perhaps expecting to find a waterway in the sky.

The final wonder of the canals is a flight of 29 pound locks on the Kennet and Avon Canal at Devizes in Wiltshire. This had numerous large side ponds to ensure that the locks did not run out of water. During the ownership of the Great Western Railway, however, the ponds were neglected and allowed to silt-up, the railway company undertaking only minor repairs. The whole system is now in a badly run-down condition, although open in parts, and is undergoing gradual restoration in the hands of a preservation group.

Chapter 8

Horse boating today

This is now mainly in the form of trips and short excursions for holiday-makers, along parts of the canal system not widely used for other purposes. Apart from the difficulties of eroded towing paths and almost non-existent stabling, there are many other excuses as to why the long anticipated revival of horse towing has become a forlorn hope. Even where the towing paths are still in reasonable condition, the horse and its towing line are scarcely popular with anglers, ramblers and owners or hirers of cabin cruisers. Since the 1950s there have been few horses on the roads and seeing them at close quarters is no longer an everyday experience for the majority of people, by whom they may now be regarded either as objects of sentiment or with suspicion and prejudice. On unexpectedly meeting a horse along the towing path many people adopt the attitude 'Whatever is it doing here, isn't this a towing path?' or 'poor thing, isn't it cruel to make it pull such a heavy boat?'. There are even well-meaning complaints to the police, RSPCA or local MPs, trying to get horse towing banned, as soon as possible. Few now seem to realise that towing paths were made for horses and that drawing a converted narrow boat with a handful of trippers is easy work, compared with the loads of coal and iron they would have hauled in former days. Unless abused or over-worked, horses appreciate the challenge of such activities, enjoying the atmosphere of being with other horses and even people. They are friendly and gregarious animals and the worst possible treatment is to leave them without work or attention, in a remote paddock for days on end, where they soon become bored.

Anglers, often taking part in competitions and matches, are now widely active along the towing paths, especially at weekends. They frequently have masses of equipment, all of which may have to be moved to make way for the towing line. Such people pay fees for the pleasure and relaxation of coarse fishing on the canal system, but often forget that boaters also have rights and were there a long time before them. Other people, enjoying a picnic or taking snapshots, are sometimes genuinely scared of horses and regard them as a potential danger, like performing wild animals, safe only under the control of their keepers. The issues are not so easy to define or as clear-cut as they at first seem, which partly explains why the idea of horse-drawn hotel boats and long excursions seemed to decline during the 1970s. In the meanwhile the British Waterways Board has

Above right *A boat horse.* **Right** *The rudder of a pleasure boat.* **Far right** *Signs and public notices, all on the Llangollen canal, 1980.*

Above and above right *Front and rear three-quarter views of a boat horse and harness, Llangollen Canal, 1980.* **Left** *Transferring the rudder (from end to end) of a pleasure boat on the same canal.*

shrugged off responsibility for keeping towing paths in good repair and, at one stage, considered a ban on horse boats or not granting further licences, but these are now issued at their discretion, taking time, place and the needs of other canal users into account.

On the Llangollen Canal, or furthermost section of the Welsh Canal, there is a service of short trips, entirely horse hauled. This has been operated by the same firm, Welsh Holiday Craft Limited, based at Chester since 1884. These were originally clinker-built craft with overlapping side planks, although more recent replacements are now smooth-sided with overhead canopies, sufficient to protect passengers from sudden rain showers. The seating is both cross- and lengthwise. The boats start from a quay near the Canal Museum at Llangollen Wharf, not far from the last turning point or winding hole on the canal. Beyond this point of navigation it is difficult for all but very small boats to turn, larger cabin cruisers—having ignored warning signs on the towing path—being forced to reverse from the canal head.

There are seasonal trips along the most beautiful part of the waterway, towards its terminus and meeting place with the River Dee, although effective navigation ends near the Chain Bridge Hotel. There is no navigable connection with the Dee, from which water is sluiced into the canal from an artificial dam known as the Horse Shoe Falls. Each trip terminates at Pentefelin Wharf or Basin, at which point the rudder is transferred to the opposite end of the craft, to save turning, each boat being double-ended. There is one horse per boat, ridden by its boy-in-charge, with a mature helmsman at the tiller. Trips leave at approximately hourly intervals, although specially arranged excursions for clubs, schools or works' outings leave promptly on the hour, as arranged. Trips are operational between April and September at weekends only, but daily throughout July and August. Long trips either eastwards to Pontcysyllte Aqueduct, or westwards to the Chain Bridge and Horse Shoe Falls, may be

A typical Welsh draught horse on the Llangollen Canal, c 1950.

booked at short notice for parties of 35 and upwards during the season. In either direction the landscape is delightfully wooded, hugging the lower slopes of foothills that rise towards a mountainous and rugged hinterland.

On the Caldon Canal in Staffordshire, which was formerly an important branch of the Trent and Mersey or Grand Trunk Canal, there are now regular horse-hauled trips in the butty *Birdswood* (a former railway owned craft) that originally paired with the motorboat, *Helen*. *Birdswood* and *Helen* belong to a husband and wife team of sign-writers and boat painters who operate over the entire system of the inland waterways. Their latest venture in horse boating is run from Froghall Wharf along the unspoilt valley of the Churnet with the crew of *Birdswood* wearing traditional costume of the 19th century canal scene. The horse, known as 'Badger' was new to the waterways when first acquired, but seemed to enjoy his work and learned quickly. The *Birdswood* seats 50 passengers and has a bar and extended cabin for cooking and catering. There are tables in the fore-part of the boat so that meals may be served in transit, based on the best of home cooking. As on the Llangollen Canal, trips are either regular services or longer excursions by arrangement.

The main trip takes about two hours (but an hour longer when meals are served), being from Froghall to the Black Lion inn at Consall Wharf, near a junction with the River Churnet. Most of this lovely valley is still inaccessible to motor traffic, being without public roads, and has become an ideal nature reserve. There is a pound lock to pass through at Flint Mill and a short tunnel near Froghall, which latter is claimed to be the lowest on the English waterways system. Working headquarters for boat trips, also containing a flat and studio, are in a former warehouse on Froghall Wharf, leased to Jaki and Bill Young by the Inland Waterways Board. This area is now very different from what it was in the old days of commercial usage, when Froghall Basin was a terminus not only of the canal but of a system of tramways, linking with extensive limestone quarries. Froghall Tunnel is without towing paths and *Birdswood* has to be shafted through, reunited with Badger at the opposite portal.

Further south, in the Home Counties, the well-known firm of 'Horse Barge' have been operating trips over the lower section of the Grand Union Canal for a number of years. The undertaking is registered at Berkhampsted and mainly works from a wharf in the area of King's Langley. The main craft involved is the *Ben Klibrech*, which may be hired from a number of starting places betwen the above mentioned points. Among other facilities are seats for 50 under weatherproof awnings, a bar, catering, a dance area for about 40 persons and the opportunity to arrange either a film show or a discotheque, as required. Horses used by this firm are of the massive shire type, perhaps the favourite—especially with children (having appeared on the BBC TV programme, *Blue Peter*)—is the mare, Patience. This animal, although having a reputation for good behaviour and gentleness, is addicted to sandwiches, which should be kept well beyond her reach.

In the heart of rural Devonshire horse-drawn trips are now run over a restored section of the Grand Western Canal, on which power boats are officially banned. The present line extends from Tiverton to Loudwell, now a haven for wildlife, especially water fowl, as these are not disturbed by the fumes, noise and excessive wash of motorboats or cabin cruisers. This was originally to have been a ship canal, linking with other waterways to connect the Bristol Channel with the English Channel and the south coast, although later utilised by limestone traffic from quarries near Tiverton. It was revived by the Devon County Council as a country park, in 1971, after 50 years of neglect and semi-abandonment. There is now a service of two horse-drawn trip boats, the *Hyades* and the *Tivertonian,* working over a lock-free section where the waters are near-transparent and the towing path is still in excellent condition. The *Tivertonian* is an 82 seater vessel while the *Hyades* takes 53 passengers. There are trips on all public holidays from the Easter period and daily from the second half of May to September. Most trips are from Tiverton to East Manley, taking 2½ hours, although on certain days the excursions are to Peverell and Burlscombe, further down the line. Drinks and light refreshments are available on board both craft. There are three heavy horses used on this line, perhaps the most popular being a shire known as Ben, frequently in charge of *Tivertonian.*

On the main line of the Shropshire Union Canal the converted narrow boat, *Iona,* makes excursions or trips from Norbury Junction to Market Drayton and other destinations. It has a bar and full catering facilities and may be hired for one hour, two hours or five hours, by arrangement. There are normally 48 passengers per trip. This service was originally handled by Shropshire Union Cruises, but has recently been taken over by the Steam Cruising Company of Norbury, Staffordshire.

On a restored section of the Kennet and Avon Canal there are two horse-drawn trip boats operating from Newbury to Hungerford, on Sundays, from Easter to September; booking is advisable. The trip takes about three hours—out and back. Other cruises are from Kintbury. Two boats, the *Avon* and the *Kennet Valley,* are involved, with three horses on the establishment, based on Greenham Island, Newbury, Berkshire. The *Avon* takes 100 passengers and the *Kennet Valley* 90 passengers. There are bar facilities on each craft.

The Chester packet Company run horse-drawn trips in the narrow boat, *Betelgeuse,* from the Tower Wharf, Chester, to either Backford or Christleton, on the Shropshire Union Canal, taking between two and three hours per trip. Services are run mainly at weekends or by special charter, with extra trips during

These pages *Three views of a pleasure trip in an ex-coal barge on the remaining section of the Glasgow Union Canal.*

the school holidays (summer period) or between Easter and mid-September. Tea, coffee and other light refreshments may be served but there are no bar facilities.

The Cromford Canal Society now run the 50 ft narrow boat, *John Gray,* over a restored section of the Cromford Canal, drawn by a single horse. Trips are on Saturdays and Sundays between April and September, taking up to 40 passengers per journey. The length of trip is 45 minutes each way, between Cromford Wharf and Leawood Pumphouse.

Pamela

During the early 1970s there were a number of holiday cruises over the inland waterways in the hotel boat, *Pamela.* This was a converted 70 ft narrow boat built at the turn of the century to work over the Birmingham and Black Country networks. It was a composite boat with sides of riveted cast-iron plating and a bottom of elm planks (later replaced by steel), in which condition she worked until the end of the 1976 boating season. She was drawn by a part-Irish draught horse named Jim, standing 16½ hands high. Jim was said to know nearly every lock, tunnel and roving bridge on 1,500 miles of canals in England and Wales, having a remarkable memory. During the season Jim covered well over a thousand miles at an average of ten to twelve miles per day, including the Grand Union Canal, the Trent and Mersey Canal, the Staffordshire and Worcester-shire Canal and many other lines. Although popular with children and older people, especially retired boaters in their waterside cottages, he earned many snide remarks from anglers—who had to remove their rods and gear at lightening speed to avoid being swept into the canal. There were also one or two minor collisions, but no serious accidents, usually with novice boaters and hirers of cabin cruisers meeting a horse boat for the first time. Further problems were encountered in finding overnight pasturage or stabling, but local farmers were mostly friendly and co-operative although some charged small grazing fees.

During 1973 *Pamela* was recognised as part of the 'Adventure Holiday Scheme' run by the Youth Hostels Association. From early in April there were weekly cruises of the canal network, shared by both members and non-members of the Association run from a wharf at Trevor on the Llangollen Canal. There were double cabins for eight passengers with a crew of three including skipper, cook and horseman. The skipper was also the helmsman or steerer. Passengers were encouraged to assist with tasks about the boat and to open locks or swing bridges. In July there was a special bird-watching cruise, organised in conjunction with the Royal Society for the Protection of Birds, the trip starting from Llangollen.

Unfortunately this service, although greatly appreciated, had to be discontinued through the deterioration of towing paths along some of the main trunk routes and the unwillingness of British Waterways Board (in the circumstances) to renew her licence or the licence of her sister craft, the *Hyades,* which latter found a new career on the revived Grand Western Canal, as previously described.

Right *'Jim' towing* Pamela, *late 1960s.*

The hotel boat, Pamela, *1968.*

Commercial boating

There is still a handful of commercial boaters on the narrow canals (mostly engaged in a seasonal coal trade) but only one professional horse boater, in the original sense. This is Caggy Stevens of Stevens and Keay, working over the Birmingham and Black Country Navigations from the Oldbury district. 'Caggy' (slang for left-handed) was born in 1918 and began working on day boats shortly after leaving school during the early 1930s. For several years he worked for an aunt, then in charge of boat steerage for the Anchor Iron Works. At the end of this period he joined his father in the family haulage business, working with a boat and two horses until Caggy's father died in 1943. He was soon committed to the important coal trade of the West Midlands, employing several hired hands and a number of boats in daily runs between the Cannock pits and factories with private wharves, then deeply involved in the war-effort.

Caggy bought his first motorboat or tug in 1947 which he used for trading as far north as Stoke-on-Trent, with five butties in tow. For local work, however, mainly collecting factory waste on the Birmingham Navigations, Caggy remained loyal to horses. In the centre of Birmingham there are many narrow locks close together and working through them with a well-trained horse is much easier than operating over the same line with motor boats. The horses owned by Caggy were famous as characters in their own right, but also as survivors—outlasting the majority of powered craft on the same line. Jean, a trusted mare, worked daily through Camp Hill and Farmer's Bridge Locks until an advanced age, leaving the waterways in 1966. She was replaced by a gelding named Mac who died in 1977, only a few months after featuring in a law suit concerning obstructions on the towing path of the Fazeley Canal, awarded in Caggy's favour. Mac was the last horse surviving from a stud which drew a large fleet of horse-drawn rubbish boats, previously owned by Birmingham Corporation. Caggy's present horse was unfortunately injured when he shied and fell into the water, simultaneously cutting his foot on broken glass, so that he had to grow a new hoof before returning to service.

As a tail-piece to the commercial side of horse boating there was an interesting movement of coal during the May 1980 celebrations (Rocket 150 Cavalcade), marking the 150th Anniversary of the Rainhill Locomotive Trials, at which Stephenson's Rocket, in establishing the supremacy of steam-worked railways, also commenced the gradual decline of both canals and horse haulage. The coal necessary for firing a replica of the Rocket used at the celebrations was mined or 'specially dug-out' at the Chatterley Whitfield Mining Museum. It was taken to the nearest wharf at Red Bull on the Trent and Mersey Canal, hauled in a wagon drawn by a pair of grey shires, owned by the National Coal Board. At Red Bull Wharf it was loaded into a restored coal boat *Phoebe* and taken by a roundabout route—due to the temporary closure of the Harecastle Tunnel—to Lymm, where it was again transferred to road transport for the final leg of its journey to Bold Colliery—the stabling point for locomotives taking part in the festival. A single vanner type horse was used throughout the canal haulage route of (with diversions) over a hundred miles.

Chapter 9

Horse-towed craft

Previous mention has been made of outstanding craft towed by horses, mules and donkeys over the inland waterways, which are here described in further detail and by regions. Only those known to have been hauled in this manner on a regular basis are discussed, excluding craft that were exclusively or mainly self-powered, bowhauled or rigged for sailing.

Arun Navigation, barges

These were used over the long-defunct Wey and Arun Navigation, linking the tidal reaches of the Thames (and London Docks) with Portsmouth, taking a shorter route than through the Straits of Dover and avoiding contact with French privateers, especially during the Napoleonic Wars. There were both sailing and horse-drawn craft, mainly working fly with few intermediate stops. The larger types, similar to Thames spritsail barges, were up to 100 tons capacity but smaller, horse-drawn types were 40, 30 and 20 tons, but usually termed barges whatever their size or capacity. They were nearly all transom-ended or squared-off at the stern, tarred black and had few or no painted decorations. Most of the smaller craft were in the hands of owner-boaters, few having more than one or two boats at a time. Barge and boat traffic on the Arun Navigation remained horse-drawn until the 1930s, but ceased by the mid-1930s. Towing was by heavy horses in tandem, with a crew of two men per boat or barge.

Basingstoke Canal

There were a number of heavy barges used on this line, mainly hauled by heavy or shire horses in tandem. These were often similar to or identical with those on the Wey Navigation, having bluff bows and transom sterns, also round bilges. Early examples were up to a capacity of 54 tons, measurements being 72 ft 6 in length and 13 ft 6 in beam. Craft of this type were first controlled by John Birnie and Company.

A.J. Harmsworth and Company ran a fleet of even larger craft from 1902 until shortly before the Second World War, most of which were constructed in a yard at Ash Vale near Aldershot. In working over the Thames, via the Wey Navigation, they were able to handle 80 tons, especially down stream from Weybridge to London Docks. Working back to Ash Vale they were limited to 50 tons. Later barges were either residential craft with a full-time crew known as 'Resos', or daytime craft (without crew quarters) known as 'Odd 'uns'—the latter used on shorter trips. Odd 'uns also lightened other barges changing from the Wey Navigation to the Basingstoke Canal proper. The last of these popular types was built in 1935 and known as *Ariel I*. Trade over the canal ceased during the 1940s.

Bridgewater and Taunton Canal, shoes

Horse-drawn boats were widely used on this navigation and were known as 'shoes'. They were up to a capacity of 5/6 tons each and drawn in trains of a dozen or more, like tub-boats. Similar craft may also have been used over the Grand Western and Chard Canals, at least during the first half of the 19th century. Their dimensions were 20 ft by 8 ft by 3 ft, usually having a high-square stern. They were used for general merchandise, quarried stone and for carrying turf fuel or withies (the latter for basketmaking).

Stroudwater Canal (Navigation), barges

These were drawn by either men or horses but, from the mid-19th century, mainly the latter. They were sturdy, almost flat-bottomed craft with a massive keelson or false keel. Some could be rigged for sailing, especially when working across or over the Severn Estuary. The measurements were 68 ft by 12 ft, with up to 50 tons capacity. Large numbers worked in the coal trade, across the Severn, via Bullo Pill or inlet. A few lasted until the mid-1930s in their original form, but were later dismasted and towed by tugs. Crew quarters were below decks in cabins fore and aft, (each barge was worked by two or three men each). Large numbers were owned by James Smart of Chalford, constructed by Gardiners of Brimscombe Port.

Trent barges

These were divided between the large down-stream and the smaller up-stream craft. Some also worked on to the adjacent Fossdyke and Witham Navigation (mainly smaller types). Those working northwards on to the Humber were often rigged for sailing, while those moving up-stream were mainly unrigged and horse-drawn. Steam tugs eventually replaced horses on all parts of the river. The average horse-drawn type was 60 ft by 11 ft, slightly larger after improvements had been made to the navigation by William Jessop (1745-1814). Capacity was about 50 tons. Most carried lee-boards for the tidal reaches, leaving these ashore when working up-stream or on to the Grantham Canal or Fossdyke. A later type of iron-hulled barge was known as a 'Nottingham Pill or Pan', mainly working between Grantham and Burton-on-Trent. The latter was square, almost straight-sided and up to 50 tons capacity.

Wey Navigation, barges

These were bluff wooden barges working over the semi-canalised Wey Navigation which were horse-drawn until 1960. They were similar to certain craft of the Arun Navigations and the Basingstoke Canal and were decked-over with hatches to cover the holds when fully loaded. Some carried lee and washboards for use on the tidal Thames. An important and characteristic feature was the large wooden rudder and tiller, the latter curved but flat on top, having a small upright peg or handle, used by the steerer as a convenient hand-grip. There were cabin or living quarters fore and aft, although the fore-cabin

A Wey Barge

was often used as a rope locker and place of general storage. There was usually a crew of three.

In the early days most barges worked between Guildford, Byfleet, Weybridge and London Docks, horse-hauled for most of their journey. In later years steam tugs replaced horses from Weybridge, down-stream. Most were up to dimensions of 73 ft by 13 ft 10½ in, although a few were slightly smaller. Capacity to a wharf at Coxes' Lock Mill was 80 tons, but much less further inland. Those working on the adjacent Godalming Canal (a continuation of the Wey Navigation) were limited by a draught of 3 ft 6 in. Nearly all craft were constructed at the Dapdune Wharf Boatyard, made and owned by William Stevens and Sons, proprietors of the Wey Navigation and the Godalming Canal. The transomed stern would be painted white, having the name of the owners in large black lettering. An important feature of the rudder on each craft was the way it could be turned back to lie flat against the stern, allowing extra space in lock pounds and for mooring purposes. It was towed by two shire horses apiece, in tandem. The towing post was a wooden or timber head at the fore-end. Most had an anchor for mooring in the tideway, raised and lowered by a windlass on the bows.

Chelmer and Blackwater, Ipswich and Stowmarket Navigations

On the Chelmer and Blackwater Navigation, opened in 1797, large wooden barges were used with dimensions of about 60 ft by 16 ft but with shallow draught. The largest were up to 27/28 tons capacity but were mostly 3 or 4 tons less. An extensive beam and flat bottom allowed them to load fairly high above the waterline. Most were bluff at the bows, square at the stern but sometimes double-ended, to save turning. Originally all-wooden craft, they were replaced by steel lighters during the early 1950s. Most traffic was connected with the

Right *A river/canal barge of the Eastern Counties under construction. From the painting by John Constable, RA.*

A passenger boat as used on the Lancaster Canal—the Crewdson.

timber trade, operated from a wharf at Chelmsford owned by Brown and Sons Limited, timber merchants and owners of a steam sawmill.

Craft on the Ipswich and Stowmarket Navigations were similar to those on the Chelmer and Blackwater, being of broad beam and shallow draught, drawing 2 ft 6 in and 3 ft, fully laden. The capacity was about 25 tons and the dimensions, 55 ft by 14 ft. So-called Gipping Barges on this waterway, also working on the Gipping Navigation, carried 30 tons each.

Lancaster Canal

Commercial or coal and freight carrying craft on this waterway were similar to some of those on the Leeds and Liverpool Canal. They worked as far north as Kendal, from Preston and its connections with the Ribble Estuary. The dimensions were 72 ft by 14 ft, carrying up to 50 tons of cargo in a hold of 5 ft depth. The laden draught was 3 ft 4 in. The horses were either singles or tandem pairs.

All types were horse-drawn rather than sailing vessels; the tall haling or hauling masts could be moved into different positions to suit the hauling team, stepped near the fore-end of each craft on the towing path side. The bows were high and bluff with a small fore-deck and larger after-deck. Wooden craft were replaced by iron-hulled vessels during the late 19th century as wooden hulls needed more repairs and attention with fewer slipping facilities in this area from the 1890s onwards. The main living quarters were in the stern which consisted of a large, square cabin with bunks fitted across the stern-end. The crews were either two men or a man and his family and the main cargoes were coal, lime, building materials and quarried stone, lasting until the late 1940s. The principal carriers were Baines Brothers and the Wigan Coal and Iron Company Limited, later followed by Ashcrofts and W. & J. Turner, although the latter soon came to rely mainly on steamers and powered craft. Most barges were decorated on the square sterns with ornate scrollwork, stars and roundels.

Horse-drawn passenger boats or packets on the Lancaster Canal, also known as Swift Boats, were very similar to an even earlier craft used on the canals of Central Scotland. They first came to Preston in 1833, there being four of almost identical design, used mainly by tourists and holiday makers bound to and from the Lake District. Perhaps the best known of these, and flagship of the small fleet, was the *Crewdson* seating 90 passengers, both first and second class. (The classes divided from each other by a bar and steward's pantry amidships.) Accommodation was mainly closed and covered but with limited seating in the open, fore and aft. The dimensions of *Crewdson* (named after a director of the canal company) were 72 ft by 6 ft by 2 ft 6 in. In later years this craft was renamed *Water Witch II* and used as a director's inspection barge.

Leeds and Liverpool Canal

Craft on this line were mainly so-called short boats. These were able to pass through 62 ft short locks between Leeds and Wigan, although from Liverpool to Wigan and over the Rufford Branch, craft at least 10 ft longer could be used—later known as long boats or barges. Long boats could also work over an enlarged section of the Leigh Branch from 1822. The beam of all craft was 14 ft 3 in maximum. Both types (long and short boats), were similar to barges, with rounded bilges, the bodywork held together by floors and frames. Most were remarkable for their colourful and highly decorative sterns, embellished with ornate patterns. The majority had square sterns but a slightly smaller fly boat had a rounded stern. Many were family boats with two cabins—one at either end. While the family occupied the stern cabin the fore-cabin was the domain of the spare hand. Stove pipes from both cabins were up to 6 ft high and could be detached for passing under low bridges and other obstructions. A short boat carried about 40 tons on a draught of 3 ft 6 in, while long boats shipped 30 tons more on a draught of 5 ft.

The Leeds and Liverpool
short boat

Victoria, *a Leeds and Liverpool Canal short boat.*

   Both short and long boats were originally all-wooden craft (with longitudinal timbers) towed by a single heavy horse. Later types were all-steel. Features of the typical horse-drawn craft would be a feed box or proven tub (provender tub) on the after deck and a water barrel (five gallons capacity) mounted on a deck-still in a sideways position. A braided rudder line, similar to the so-called swan's neck on working boats of the narrow canals, was a woven length of coloured cord leading from the stern post to the top of the rudder blade.

The Bridgewater Canal

Most of the heavy commercial craft on this line, used for freight or minerals, were known as flats. They were decked-over and often capable of traversing both still water navigations and the tidal reaches of the Rivers Mersey and Weaver. Undecked barges, in a minority, were also known as lighters. Dimensions of the so-called Manchester (horse-drawn) flats, would be about 71 ft by 14 ft 3 in, able to carry 80 tons on a draught of 3 ft 6 in. Most types were known as 'Dukers', in honour of the third Duke of Bridgewater (the Canal Duke and sponsor of the navigation) who owned 60 flats and 46 barges or lighters, plus a number of narrow boats, at the time of his death in 1803. Horses met the incoming craft from the tidal Mersey at the top of Runcorn Locks, a traffic later monopolised by steam tugs known as 'Little Packets' or (less frequently) 'Jack Sharps'. Tanker barges, with a high stern cabin, drawn by horses or mules, were known as 'floats'. Most horse-drawn craft were wooden-hulled with a crew of two men or a man and a boy. Some, however, were family boats or barges.

Special flats designed for canal work only were unrigged and towed by two horses apiece, although smaller craft were drawn by single horses or mules. The estuarine type needed at least two heavy horses each. The largest type of inland barge or 'cut flat' would be 68 ft long and 14 ft 9 in beam, carrying about 80 to 90 tons on a 5 ft draught. The towing or hailing mast was stepped almost amidships and known as the 'neddy'. Some of the cut flats were family boats but most were crewed by two men or a captain and mate. So-called 'Rochdale Flats' worked over the Rochdale Canal from Liverpool and Manchester, and were mainly used for carrying bales of cotton to mills in that area as they had narrow side-decking round the cargo hold to take extra bales.

Passenger boats on the Bridgewater Canal ran from about 1767, the first service operated between Manchester and Altrincham, although later was extended with the progress of the main line to Lymm and Runcorn Docks. At Runcorn there were connections with other craft (sailing vessels and later steamers) to the Mersey Ports, although passengers had to walk from the canal (top) lock to the river wharf at a much lower level, via a pathway down the lock shoulder. Early packet or passenger boats may well have been converted coal barges, each pulled by a single horse. Although mules may have been used experimentally, these were not as swift or as reliable for this type of work as horses. In 1774 two purpose-built packet boats were introduced, these being almost identical and the fore-runners of a whole fleet of such craft. They had a saloon or stateroom for refreshments and a number of first, second and third class cabins. They were towed by two horses or more in tandem which were ridden by postillions. The average trip time was eight hours between a wharf in Manchester and Runcorn Docks. Food and drink were served on the move but there were also a number of short stops at wayside inns.

Humber craft

This type would consist mainly of keels, some large enough for estuarine or even coastwise trade. When working inland over the Aire and Calder or Calder and

The horse float, Cedar, *as used on the Bridgewater Canal.*

A West Country keel

Hebble Navigations they were frequently drawn by two or more horses, hired for the purposes. Larger types were about 78 ft 6 in in length with a beam of 14 ft 6 in and a capacity between 80 and 100 tons. When fully rigged for tidal reaches they had large square sails and resembled the Viking Long Ships—but with higher freeboard—from which they may have descended. Smaller or Western barges were all-wooden craft, towed by a single horse apiece. Each barge was 58 ft long, having two cabins, the fore-cabin (in the bows) serving as a galley. They were either family craft or crewed by two men. Non-tidal keels were mainly restricted to the Aire and Calder Navigations west of Goole.

The Fenland waterways

Lighters were used on the Fenland waterways at least from the 17th century. Early types were either bowhauled, square-rigged or towed by horses. Towards the end of the 19th century the average lighter was recognised as an all-wooden craft towed by a horse of the shire type. Dimensions of each craft were 42 ft by 10 ft, having a capacity of 25 tons on a draught of 3 ft 6 in. The majority of such vessels were double-ended and flat-bottomed, very light for their size, with a draught of 12 in empty. Some were decked, with hatch covers over the cargo space, but most were open, using tarpaulins in wet weather. They were mostly roped and chained together in gangs or runs of four, each run drawn by a single horse. The run was given a certain amount of support and rigidity by the use of a wooden beam or jambing pole between each craft, linking them together and reinforcing other connections. The second boat usually had a small cabin for two men and was known as the 'house' or 'houselighter'. The horse boy or horse knocker slept in a coop-like structure on one of the following craft, usually the third boat. The rear of the run or gang was brought up by a pram, tender or 'cock boat', usually a small dinghy. Most gangs also had a special lighter or 'horse boat' to ferry the horse across where the towing path changed sides without roving bridges. On certain runs, especially when the navigation followed a twisting course, the towing line would be a rope of 480 ft, although normally about 100 ft. When poling or shafting was necessary this would be done with a long boathook, known in the Fens as a 'sprit'.

The towing harness was similar to that used on other waterways but the leads to the spreader or track stick joined together about 5 ft from the rearward harness then continued a further 2 ft to end with a hook and eye attachment for the actual towing line. Some craft, larger than average, also working on to the Great Ouse, were 70 ft by 14 ft with a capacity of 70 tons on a 3 ft 6 in draught. There were also much smaller 'Ouse Lighters' with a capacity of 8 or 9 tons.

The Suffolk Stour

Craft on this waterway were similar to Fenland lighters and worked in pairs, connected by a 30 ft long coupling pole or steering pole, each pair drawn by a single horses. They were double-ended vessels, often of sturdy build with clinker or overlapping side planks. A typical example measured 46 ft 9 in long by 10 ft 6 in beam, with a depth of 3 ft 2 in. Each craft carried 13 tons on a draught of 2 ft 5 in or 26 tons behind a single horse, although two horses were frequently needed for up-stream traffic against the current.

The towing post or attachment was in a hollow near the centre of the craft, known as the 'steerer's well'. Most craft in later years were owned by the River Stour Navigation Company, carriers on their own line. Each craft was usually in the care of two men and a boy or two men only. All commercial traffic ceased on this line about 1928.

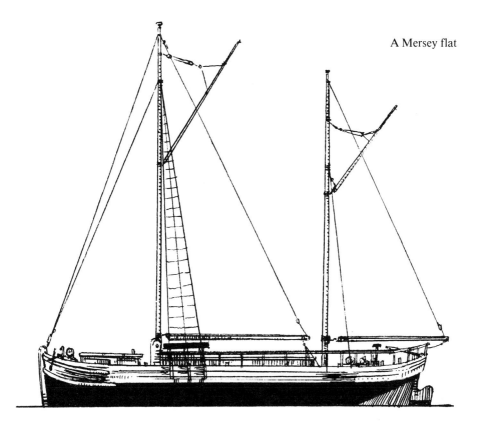

A Mersey flat

An empty Glamorgan Canal Company boat at the canal locks, Pontypridd

South Wales, narrow boats

The horse-hauled craft on the isolated waterways of South Wales and Monmouthshire, not connected with other parts of the system, were mainly day boats. Some carried general merchandise but most were engaged in the coal and iron trades of the industrial valleys. They were mostly all-wooden boats with a small stern cabin or shelter aft, in which the crew of two men or a man and a boy, might sleep away from their home-base at least two nights running, although this was unusual. Horizontal side planks on Glamorgan Canal boats were five in number, while those on the Brecknock and Abergavenny navigations were only four per side. Cabins were less frequently seen on the so-called 'open boats' of the Neath, Swansea and Tennant Canals. The stem of most craft appeared to incline slightly forwards in a convex or bow-shape.

In later years the stove pipes on boats with cabins were made very short, as mining subsidence often lowered the height of over-bridges. Dimensions were 60 ft by 8 ft 6 in, carrying 20 tons on a draught of 2 ft 9 in over the Glamorganshire, Monmouthshire and Brecknock and Abergavenny lines, but 60 ft by 9 ft on the Neath and Tennant Canals, loading to 24 tons on the same draught. Boats on the Swansea Canal were 65 ft by 7 ft 6 in carrying about 20 tons on 2 ft 9 in draught. The majority of canal craft in South Wales remained horse-drawn until the late 1930s and the period of closure.

Narrow boats on the canals of the Midlands

These were of many varieties, able to appear on most canal or river navigations, throughout the country, apart from the Leeds and Liverpool Canal (between

A typical narrow boat (family boat) near Watford, Grand Union Canal.

Wigan and Leeds) and the Huddersfield Broad Canal. They were usually of dimensions (approximately 72 ft long and just under 7 ft beam, conforming to the lock pounds of most narrow canals, also to the narrow passages through bridgeholes. Those apparently designed by James Brindley for his own navigations, were slightly smaller at about 70 ft by 6 ft with a capacity of 25 tons on a draught of 2 ft 6 in. Such craft were to be pulled by a single medium-sized horse in the care of two men or a man and a boy. Sometimes two boats were used with either a single horse of the heavier type, two mules, a pair of donkeys or a mule and a horse. The idea of pairs or longer trains was soon abandoned, however, in favour of one horse per boat, at least until the days of steam tugs and other forms of mechanical haulage. Such boats were of all-wooden construction and fairly low in the water, especially when loaded, having a small living cabin at the stern-end, while the tiller had a pronounced upward curve, similar to the way it appeared in the reversed position on later narrow boats.

Early canal boats were known to have a strong resemblance to open coal boats or 'starvationers', used on the underground waterways of the Duke of Bridgewater's colliery at Worsley, especially regarding their sturdy build and pronounced guards or side strakes. Most were double-ended, like the day boats of the Birmingham navigations. Other prototype narrow boats, on perhaps more generous lines, were said to have been designed by a canal haulier named Monk of Tipton, near the turn of the century, this type henceforth known as 'Monkey Boats', especially in the West Midlands.

During the first 20 years of the 19th century the haulage firm of Messrs Pickfords produced a fleet of standard craft for the narrow canals, far superior to anything used up to that time. These had larger cabins and greater depth of cargo space, the cargoes lashed-down and protected by cloths or sheets to give the laden boat a tent-like appearance. By the mid-19th century a familiar modern type had emerged with upright stands, cratch or frontboard and a high towing mast (often in two or more telescopic sections), well forward. The stands, mast and a number of narrow side struts usually supported a gangway of top planks between the fore-end and the stern cabin, raised well above the cabin roof by means of a near-triangular cabin block.

Wooden boats were mainly built from the 1760s to the period shortly before the First World War, although a few were still being made until the 1950s. In later years, however, knees or inner brackets connecting bottom and side planks were made of iron. Later iron and steel boats or composite boats had metal sides and wooden (elm) bottoms, but were frequently associated in this style with the internal combustion engine and the motorboat rather than horse-drawn craft.

Although the average horse-drawn narrow boat, from the mid-19th century, was a 70 footer and upwards, smaller and slightly narrower craft worked over the Huddersfield Narrow Canal, Sir John Ramsden's Canal and the waters of the Calder and Hebble Navigations. In later years, towards the end of the horse and mule towing era, former horse boats were often drawn by a motor or steam-powered craft and known as 'butties'. A pair of butties or a butty and tug were also known as 'Joshers', which was Black Country slang for old pals or workmates. It has been further claimed, however, that 'Josher' further relates

A typical narrow boat (family boat) at the entrance to Blisworth Tunnel, Grand Union Canal.

to the christian name of one of the founders of the firm of Fellows, Morton and Clayton Limited, this being Joshua Clayton.

Narrow boats navigating over rivers and tidal waters were seldom towed by horses but either hauled by tugs in trains or rigged with a jury or temporary mast and sailed, at least for short distances. They were frequently breasted-up or lashed side by side, on rivers, as this made them less vulnerable to tides, currents or wash from larger craft. Such navigations, however, were always restricted by local conditions of tide and weather.

Day boats

Perhaps the best known of these operated in the Birmingham and Black Country areas, although similar types were also to be found in South Wales (as previously described), the Staffordshire Potteries and East Lancashire. At one time they may well have been the largest single type of boat used on the inland waterways, throughout the country. Many were open and either cabinless or had a mere shelter rather than a full-sized cabin or cuddy. They were always narrow and low in the water, having fairly straight sides without much flare. Most were double-ended, the rudder post near upright and the rudder transferable from one end to the other. Sometimes rudders were unshipped and taken from one boat to another, at the end of a day's stint, dragged overland by the boat horse. In this connection it may be noted that there were few turning or winding places on the Birmingham Navigations, due to the shortage of space in built-up areas.

A better-shaped, more substantial day boat with the rudder fixed at one end only, carried a variety of cargoes, although most were related to the needs of the iron and coal trades. In later years a number of day boats were used for collecting factory waste, domestic rubbish and other scrap or salvage. The towing mast, especially on Birmingham day boats and coal boats, could be chained to a crosswise fore-mast beam or middle beam, and made to lean at an angle towards the towing path, useful for clearances under low bridges when the boat was empty and high in the water. One of the most familiar types was the Birmingham coal boat, with minimum vertical features, later towed in runs or trains by tugs.

The so-called 'hot-holers' were iron or steel craft working into the basins of forges and foundries, while the 'Rowley Raggers' were stone boats under contract to granite quarries of Rowley Regis and Dudley—rag being a form of stone, broken small and used in road making and repairing. Railway or station boats, the former slightly larger than the latter, were horse hauled until the 1950s and either wooden or iron-hulled craft, serving the railway owned canal and interchange basins, once familiar in all parts of the Black Country—being under cover and having wharfside access for both railway and road vehicles. Railway boats were of superior construction, compared with other day boats, mainly operated by the London and North Western Railway, the Midland Railway and later by their successor the London, Midland and Scottish Railway, in parts not widely or directly served by their main lines. Other similar boats were operated—in the Wolverhampton area—by Thomas Bantocks and Sons, acting as road and canal transport agents for the Great Western Railway. After nationalisation in 1948 they worked mainly under contract to the Western Region of British Railways. They were mainly keelless craft, low in the water

A day boat (horse boat) on the Staffordshire and Worcestershire Canal.

but with exceptionally long knees or inner brackets of the cargo space. The sides were often partly of iron (for the upper sections, to the gunwales) and partly of wood—to connect with the wooden bottoms.

The average day boat loaded to 40 tons (but usually 10 or 15 tons less), much depending on the level of the water, which may have been very shallow and silted-up on some branches. Cross timbers above the cargo space on these boats were known as fore, middle, stern-middle and bulkhead beams that helped to reinforce the structure and hold it together. The towing mast or post was a solid length of wood up to 9 ft long, fixed either in a socket of the keelson or chained to the middle beam, as previously described. It was not (unlike the mast of long distance boats) constructed in sections. Side guards to protect the fore and stern-ends of the boat were solid timbers reinforced with steel or iron strip. Later iron boats had all-metal guards.

The cost of the average day boat on the open market was very cheap, only the least expensive wood being used, such as imported deal—especially for the side planks—the standard of finish also lacking the quality of other boats and barges on the inland waterways. Towards the end of the 19th century a day boat could be bought for as little as £40, while to order a new boat—up to the period of the First World War—would be in the region of £90. This price increased during the 1930s from £120 to £150. The iron types were less popular than might have been expected as wooden craft were so cheap and turned out in such large numbers—almost mass-produced. Some boats were composites with elm-bottoms and iron sides, that might have been more expensive than the general run of contemporary craft. Decks were narrow or non-existent, the steerer perched on a cross-plank in the well of the stern, his feet only a short distance below the gunwales. Cabin space was meagre and seldom more than 4 ft long by 6 ft wide. The interior had cross and side benches, known as beds, a folding table and what became known as a 'bottle stove' (being bottle-shaped). There was also a shelf or two and perhaps a corner cupboard for dry goods such as tea and sugar. The main purpose of the cabin was to provide shelter at mealtimes and a place to brew-up or boil a kettle.

The main haulage firms, mines, factories or forges using narrow (day) boats, sometimes employed their own crews but more frequently contracted out either to casual labour or to agents employing them, known as steering companies. Work, especially during the late 19th and early 20th centuries, varied from day to day and attracted a tough, coarse-grained individual, quite different from the long distance boaters—the latter being men with a greater sense of security and responsibility. There were two men per boat, with one in charge of the horse and the other at the tiller. There were a few women steerers during the First World War, but these were in a small minority—mainly working for family firms. On the whole the Birmingham Canal Navigations were a man's world with bare-knuckle fights on the towing paths and feats of physical strength and fool-hardiness in most wayside taverns nearly every night of the week. Dog fights, cock fights and killing rats against time, were common-place pastimes.

At the end of the day or shift, boaters frequently changed from one boat to another, or even to a different line of navigation, retaining the horse (which would be needed to tow the larger objects), rudder, mast, tiller, water can, feed tin, hay net and fire bucket. The latter was a large can with holes punched in the sides, used in or with the cabin stove.

Northern boats

These mainly worked in South Lancashire and the North Midlands, some appearing on the Leeds and Liverpool Canal, also on the Bridgewater Canal and other navigations. They had fairly deep or six plank sides with a length of 62 ft. The fore-ends tended to be squat and wedge-shaped and capacity was about 30 tons. Some were double-ended, well-pointed at both ends, although this changed to a counter stern when large numbers were converted from horse-drawn to power boats, about 1914. They were often built in the yard of Simpson Davis and Company of Runcorn.

So-called pottery boats on the Trent and Mersey Canal traded in general goods but were frequently involved in the carriage of crated china or earthenware. To make them more adaptable for this purpose they appeared to be barrel-shaped with rounded bilges. When empty or lightly loaded they tended to roll. Many of these were owned by the Anderton Company and built by the same firm at their Longport Depot. The crews, in common with other boaters on this line, were known as 'knobsticks'.

River Severn boats

Narrow boats working over the River Severn and adjacent waterways, were known as long boats or 'Severners'. They were about 72 ft long and 7 ft 2 in beam with a draught of 3 ft 9 in, fully loaded. Most were worked as singles, drawn by horses, mules or donkeys, especially pairs of donkeys when steering on to the Worcester and Birmingham Canal, from Diglis Lock, Worcester. They worked down-stream to Gloucester and frequently found their way up the Stroudwater Navigation via the Gloucester and Sharpness Canal. In later years they were frequently breasted-up in runs or pairs behind a steam tug. They were noted for their straight sides and square section.

Shrewsbury Canal boats

These were craft about 70 ft long and 6 ft 2 in beam, up to a capacity of 18 tons, but seldom loading above 16 tons. The stern cabins were fairly low with a shallow tumblehome or sloping sides for the sake of low bridges, for which the stove pipes and other uprights could be removed. They were known as 'Trench', 'Fly' or 'Reserve' Boats. Reserve boats were for local or internal traffic only, while Fly or Trench Boats often worked on to other parts of the inland waterways, especially the main line of the Shropshire Union Canal. The name Trench derives from an inclined plane on this canal up to which the boats of that name navigated.

Tar or gas boats

These were specially constructed tankers used to convey tar, ammonia water (gas water) and creosote from the local gasworks, many of which had private basins, to various industrial concerns. They were roughly the same dimensions as other narrow boats working over the Birmingham and Black Country Navigations, often comprising an iron or steel tank surrounded by a wooden shell or casing, boarded over at the top for better insulation. The inner part of the tank had swill boards to limit movements of the liquid cargo. A few were of iron construction, but the majority were wood. They were mainly divided between short haul or day boats painted all-black and known as 'black boats', and the long distance or family boats with colourful stern cabins. Some family boats reached as far north as Ellesmere Port and the Manchester Ship Canal. The majority had a small fore-cabin, approaching which would be a place for the feed barrel in a tent-like structure known as the 'cratch'. It was a common practice to load a mule or horse-drawn boat of this type two inches down by the head, which came up level under towage.

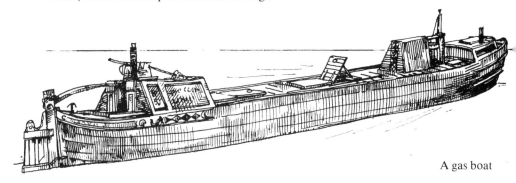

A gas boat

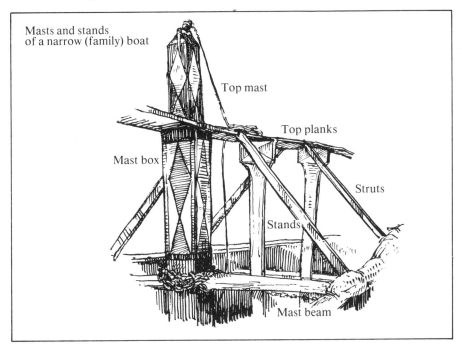

Masts and stands of a narrow (family) boat

Top mast

Top planks

Mast box

Struts

Stands

Mast beam

Family boats

There were family versions of many craft on the inland waterways, including the Lancaster Canal barges, Leeds and Liverpool short boats and several other previously discussed. What, however, may be termed the classical boats of this type were narrow or long boats working over the narrow canals, on long distance or intermediate hauls, of which about 80 per cent would—at one time—be occupied by a married couple and their family. The father was captain while his wife was first mate and the older children—making themselves useful from a very early age—were crew, working for pocket money. It may be noted that the person in charge of a boat or working pair was entitled to be known as 'Captain', this being an official rather than a courtesy title. Family boating was rare but not unknown during the early days of canals, but later adopted as an economy measure, especially from the 1850s; until by the end of the century there were over 100,000 men, women and children living and working on canal craft. There were about 19,200 boats working over 4,800 miles, at a peak period. With the increase of railway competition and cuts in wages or earnings, the average boater could no longer afford the rent or upkeep of a cottage on the land and took his dependents into the boats. Some of the owner-boaters also employed an extra hand, perhaps the younger son of a friend, who helped with heavy and dirty cargoes, sleeping in a fore-cabin, sometimes known as a rope locker. Such persons would be paid so much per trip and all found.

The stern or main living cabin of the average family boat was about 10 ft long and nearly as wide as the boat, fitted-out with a cross-bed at one end, folding into a cupboard (bedhole) during the daytime, with side-benches that could be converted into bunks for children. When the cross-bed was down this would be divided from the rest of the cabin by a curtain—the part it occupied known as

The stern cabin of a butty
(looking inwards)

the 'bedroom'. A folding table fitted over the front of the crock cupboard and was lowered at meal times, supported at the front by an under-prop. Just inside the cabin entrance or 'hatches', at the left-hand side, would be a combined cooking and heating stove, often on a raised platform. This would have a large side oven with spaces on the top for saucepans and kettles. It replaced the smaller 'bottle stove' which was mainly for heating, but was retained well into the 20th century on day boats and certain railway boats. It was possible, however, to boil a pot or kettle on a bottle stove by means of a trivet or firebar that could be swivelled into the heart of the fire by manual adjustment. Most of the cabin interior was grained and varnished or painted with colourful side-panels, on which decorative curtains in crocketwork and rows of lace plates hung. The latter were not sold exclusively to boaters but collected by them, often as souvenirs of holidays or as keepsakes. Others were manufactured cheaply in Central Europe, until the period between the world wars, and sold either in canalside shops or on market stalls, sometimes second hand. Their main features would be openwork frets round the rims or borders through which coloured ribbons could be threaded for hanging and display purposes.

Other cabin ornaments, appearing both on the cabin walls and in the crock cupboards, would be miniature windlass handles (in brass or polished steel), china ornaments such as standing figures, and horse brasses. Oil lamps served both a functional and decorative purpose, secured by curved and fluted brackets, with an elaborate shade, the latter also adorned by a miniature portrait of a member of the Royal Family or other celebrity, in cameo-form.

Most family boats were kept in immaculate condition, the brasses and fire irons polished at least twice a week. Those not seeming to care about the environment and neglecting their living quarters were known as 'Rodney Boaters' or slum dwellers of the cut. Such people were not as a rule from traditional boating or canal families but casual labour, persuaded to work a run-down narrow boat for a cut in wages, when other work was scarce.

Exterior parts of the family boat were decorated with brass rims and fittings, especially on the stove pipe, and also had well-scrubbed or pipe-clayed ropework and cordage. The latter was seen at its best and most effective on the rudder or ram's head, consisting of a lanyard-like rope connecting rudder blade and rudder post, known as the 'swan's neck', also a turban-like binding of the rudder post and sometimes the tiller, known as a 'Turk's Head'. This latter was so-named as it resembled the head-dress of an ancient Turkish warrior or janissary.

The style of painting and lettering was an important feature of both external and internal decoration, especially from the mid-19th century, when family boating first became popular. The main subject for both panels and utensils, such as dippers and watercans, would be 'roses and castles'. These were first painted by the boaters themselves, especially the owner-boaters or number-ones, but later by trained men in the boatyards when craft docked for overhaul or repairs. Day boats in the Black Country were painted with motifs of a geometrical or abstract character, but soon became battered and dirty as day boaters were less particular than family men, also less likely to remain in charge of the same boat for more than a few days at a time. On some canals, especially in the West Midlands or on the Trent and Mersey Canal, paintings of flowers were naturalistic and life-like rather than decorative (the knobstick tradition),

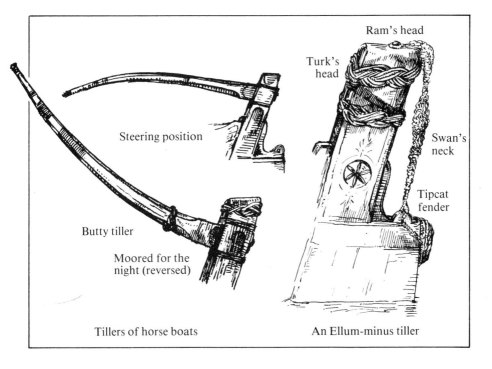

Ram's head

Turk's head

Steering position

Swan's neck

Tipcat fender

Butty tiller

Moored for the night (reversed)

Tillers of horse boats   An Ellum-minus tiller

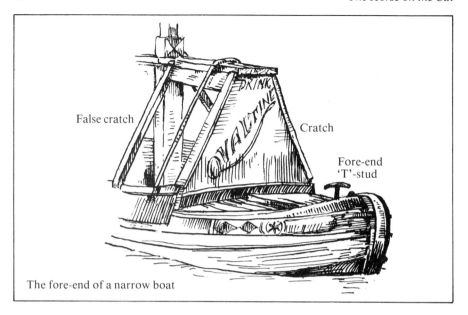

False cratch

Cratch

Fore-end
'T'-stud

The fore-end of a narrow boat

while haystacks, farm cottages and country scenes were more popular than moated castles in romantic settings. It may be noted that castles were usually of an Eastern or Balkan appearance having little in common with the mediaeval castles and grim keeps of Western Europe. While this may seem fortuitous and a mere accident of design, some claim it to be proof of the gypsy ancestry of the first boaters, many of whom came to Western countries from the Balkans and the Levant. There are various styles of painting as easy to identify as personal handwriting, especially designs on the water cans and dippers. In later years, after the Second World War, the art declined and the Inland Waterways Executive even encouraged the use of transfers.

Scows

These were container boats mainly appearing on the waterways of Central and Lowland Scotland. They were about 60 ft long and 13 ft 6 in beam, but were a foot narrower on the Monkland Canal. Capacity was up to 80 tons. Three men worked each boat, one in charge of the horse, the other steering and the third man to open locks or swing bridges, also to assist with loading and various odd jobs. Those in the coal trade could take 14 small wagons or tubs of broken coal, while others carried market carts (fully laden), livestock and general farm produce. The crew quarters were under-decked areas at the stern end, although some had a fore-cabin in the bows, also decked over. Towing was from a stud or loop on the fore-deck, the horse being a heavy-weight Clydesdale or 'Clyde'. Most craft were round bilged, double-ended and fairly low in the water. Early types were all-wooden, but from the 1820s there was a change to iron-hulled craft that moved even more swiftly through the water.

The typical packet boat on the same navigations was known as a 'gig' or swift boat, and were the prototypes for many of similar design, used in other parts of Britain. South of the Border they were known as 'Scotch Boats'. Such boats have been described in the section of this chapter dealing with craft of the Lancaster Canal. A few experimental types were made without windows.

Wide boats

These were enlarged versions of the standard narrow boat, up to 72 ft in length but from 9 ft to 11 ft beam. They could work on any canals with wider than average locks but were discouraged on several navigations as they tended to plane-up, block tunnels and cause congestion on busy lines. They were mainly general carriers but were sometimes used as tankers for bulk liquids, especially on the southern reaches of the Grand Union Canal. The sides were well rounded to save space. On the Kennet and Avon Canal they were known as 'mules' and on the northern waterways as 'bastards' or 'bastard boats'—perhaps due to the inconvenience they caused—seeming something of a cross between an ordinary narrow boat and a barge proper. At first sight they closely resembled the narrow boat, having an elaborately painted stern cabin with inward sloping tumblehome, and the cargo space often clothed-up on a structure of masts, stands and struts. They were drawn by a single horse apiece, usually of the shire type or one of the other heavy breeds. The crew would be two men (master and mate), although a few craft were family boats, rejoicing in the extra space available for the stern cabin. The upright stove pipe of the living quarters had numerous brass rims or rings. In general terms there seemed to be more brasswork on stove pipes in the south of England than on northern canals and waterways. A typical run for such a boat would be with a cargo of heavy burning

A wide boat on the Kennet and Avon Canal.

(fuel) oil, from Limehouse Docks to glass works at Alperton on the Paddington Arm or Canal. This was a 15-mile journey which took a day and a half in each direction.

Black Country wharf boats

Although previously mentioned these were outstanding craft of their type, and should not be omitted from a general survey. Also known as 'Ampton' or Wolverhampton Boats, working over a lock-free stretch of canal north of that town, so that its dimensions could be increased to between 80 and 86 ft by 7 ft 9 in. The cargo space had a maximum depth of 3 ft 9 in, able to handle up to 50 tons of coal at a given time. They were drawn by a single horse, although later in pairs or trains by tugs.

Maintenance craft

These were usually drawn by horses but, in later years bowhauled (especially over short distances), with the running down of the horse departments on the nationalised waterways. They include the horse-drawn icebreakers or rocking boats, previously mentioned, and a number of work boats or flats used in general repair and maintenance projects. While some were purpose built and resembled square-headed or swim-ended lighters, but with a lock-up cabin at one end (also used as a store-room and office), others were converted narrow boats of the standard type. Some were fitted with spoon-type ladles amidships and used for dredging operations, while others were mounted with an arched-section of stiff bristles on a curved framework, gauged to the contours of tunnels or bridgeholes and known as 'tunnel-brushing boats'. In the latter connection it may be noted that tunnels soon became caked with soot, not only from cabin stove pipes but from the funnels of steam-powered tunnel tugs, of which there were large numbers from the 1870s to the early 1930s. Such craft would be drawn by horses from the maintenance yard or depot to the nearest portals of the tunnel to be cleaned, but shafted through the interior or handled by a slow-moving tug, beyond this point.

Chapter 10

Domestic animals on the waterways

Dogs of different kinds have been kept on boats and barges from time immemorial. Although frequently a pet or children's plaything, they were also valued as guard and watch dogs. In Europe there is a special breed of German origin known as the Spitz, mainly associated with life of the inland waterways. The Dutch barge dog, similar in appearance to the Chow, is known as the Keeshund or favourite/pet dog, which spends most of its life afloat.

On the old Thames and Medway sailing barges of the spritsail type, the crew were frequently a man, a boy and their dog, the latter proving as much a member of the company as either of its companions. The dog, with the natural alertness of a healthy animal, would be on watch at all hours, warding off any intruder or sneak thief.

When canal boaters had to be away from their floating homes for a short time dogs would be left in charge, usually in the stern cabin. They were often Yorkshire terriers as these would be small enough for confined quarters, but had a loud bark which frightened strangers and were almost fearless. Dogs were normally kept in the forecabin or in kennels on top of the stern cabin, and given the freedom of the boat while others slept. They could leap ashore for further exercise and frequently enjoyed a dip in the canal on hot days.

Many dogs were lurchers (part collie and part greyhound), able to assist their masters in poaching expeditions. The odd rabbit, partridge or pheasant all added variety to the menu, many of the main line canals running through ideal sporting country. It was the dread that people working on canals might make serious inroads into their game preserves that led so many of the traditional land-owners to oppose canal construction.

Some dogs with soft mouths, obviously retrievers but sometimes other breeds, were actually trained to steal eggs from the nests of wild ducks or moorhens from backwaters and hens or ducks from farmyards. There was always the stray hen, in free range flocks, with the odd desire to lay in secret places; if these could be found it was usually by a canal boater's dog, able to sniff them out as though by instinct. Some boat dogs with a light touch could carry two eggs at a time, without mark or crack. Left to its own devices the boater's dog could usually look after itself, able to overtake the boat at any hour of day or night. Sometimes it would go missing for a day or two, but was heard scratching at the hatches (cabin doors) when least expected.

While a few boater's wives may have chosen cats as pets, and there have been many of these on sea-going ships and coastwise barges, they tended to be few and far between on the inland waterways. Cats, apart from a rare species of oriental fishing cat, normally detest water or even rain and damp weather. While there was always plenty of space and shelter on shipboard, this was certainly lacking on narrow boats, and it must have been widely recognised that normal cats would be out of their element travelling on the cut. The nearest many boaters came to owning a cat (or being owned by one) was in retirement, when they moved into a canalside cottage and were adopted by a stray. On the whole, boaters seemed to prefer dogs—the world of animal lovers, according to some authorities, being divided between cat and dog enthusiasts. L.T.C. Rolt in his *Narrow Boat* recalls seeing 'an old lady at Brentford who had a great tabby cat, wearing a collar, which was stalking about the cabin roof with mincing steps . . . while she stood at the tiller'. He further records, however, that: 'A dog is a far more common companion . . . and most boatmen seemed to find room for a kennel somewhere in the cargo space'.

Both chickens and rabbits were kept in coops and hutches, either on the stern cabin roof or in the otherwise deserted fore-cabin. The caged rabbit, bred in captivity, was either a child's pet or fattened for the pot, where boaters were not enterprising enough to set their own snares.

Chickens, kept for new-laid eggs, were very quick in adapting themselves to life afloat, and at one time were frequently encountered on the waterways of the Midlands. When a boat was delayed for loading, unloading or stoppages of any kind, they would be released from their confined quarters and taken ashore. Here they would peck about in search of natural food on any wharfside or patch of nearby wasteland. Where there were towing horses there would always be a slight spillage from nose cans, enough to provide several hens with a tasty snack. No one bothered to watch over the poultry, although they may have been rounded-up when the boat was ready to leave. As a rule the odd shout or rattle of stones in a tin can would be enough to recall them, when they would allow themselves to be shut away without further trouble. A stray hen left behind followed the boat across country almost as fast as a dog, flapping through hedges and fences, knowing just where to take short cuts, often waiting at the next lock or road bridge to jump into the cargo space.

Cage birds were often kept on canal boats, ranging from wild song birds, trapped or snared by the boaters, especially in the early days, to more exotic varieties. Large and often elaborate cages of brasswork frequently appeared on stern cabin roofs, at least up to the period of the Second World War. Canaries, linnets, bullfinches and later budgerigars (first known in Britain as Australian Love Birds), all had their spells of popularity. Although taken inside at night and sometimes allowed the freedom of the cabin after the doors had been safely shut, they spent most of their lives in the fresh air, shielded from sun and wind by a crochetwork cover over the top of the cage, usually made by the boater's wife.

Employees of the canal authorities such as lock keepers and lengthsmen, living in waterside cottages, were almost as isolated from the nearest community—in some cases—as the boaters and bargees. While keeping cats, dogs and other household pets according to whim, chickens and pigs were a necessity of rural life. Most lock keepers had large gardens and orchards, even if these tended to be of a linear character, long rather than wide. Most would have a pigsty, feeding a pig or two on household scraps and kitchen waste. Some lock keepers were also known to have kept goats, usually tethered, although some strayed on to the towing paths, grazing on herbage forbidden to canal horses and mules by strict bylaws. Geese and poultry also escaped on to the towing paths through gaps in the hedge or netting of their pens. Whatever animals or birds lived as pets on the inland waterways they usually seemed contented and well-cared for, kept only by those genuinely interested in their well-being.

Wild life—fishes, birds and beasts

The four most popular fish to be found in the waters of canals are bream, perch, rudd and roach, especially the latter. Eels are also present, using the waterways when migrating towards the sea. On most inland waterways fishing from the boats was unrestricted, but not the setting of night lines, while eels were harpooned with tridents or spears. Amphibians include newts, frogs and toads, while on the banks of the Selby Canal in Yorkshire (part of the Aire and Calder Navigations) the author recalls seeing numerous tiny lizards about an inch or two in length. All the popular varieties of wild birds are still plentiful, including some of the more exotic species. Backwaters and abandoned or little used lines are ideal nature reserves and nesting sites for kingfisher, heron, wild duck and other water fowl. Moorhens have always been plentiful where there is sufficient cover in reed beds, some of these artificially planted in so-called 'shelving sections', to break the wash of passing boats at corners and on curves. Water rats, water voles and even foxes—the latter attracted by the voles and rats as natural prey—are frequently heard but seldom seen.

"Poor Old Horse"

A number one came a bacca-ing, and they say so, and they hope so,
And we said, 'Oh Mam, that horse will die, oh, poor old horse.'

At Exhall wharf they go to load, and they say so, and they hope so,
And then he comes out on the London Road, oh, poor old horse.

Oh, he'll work all night and he'll work all day, and they say so, and
they hope so,
Put him on the inside and he'll bacca away, oh, poor old horse.

From Atherstone to Heart's Hill length, and they say so, and they
hope so,
Twas there that poor beast broke his strength, oh, poor old horse.

And after years of such abuse, and they say so, and they hope so,
You're salted down for sailors' use, oh, poor old horse.

Appendices

Gleanings

I From a notebook belonging to an employee of the Grand Union Canal Company, dating back to 1903

The extracts mainly relate to the Regent's Canal, London, later controlled by the GUC.

Downes. Stableboy. City Road Lock. Wages for trial period. 10/- per week. Increase [in red] 1/- per week from 26.9.03. 1/- per week from 3.10.04.

Horse clipping. 2/6d paid to J. Long 1st Oct 1918, for each horse.

Ice Barge. Sunday 26.1.07. 3 drivers from City Road Stables paid 4/6d beer money (men employed on ice barge to be allowed 6d per day beer money), per Mr G. [Mr Glass]. 10.1.08.

Smith. Blacksmith's Labourer (doorman), wages 3/8d per day. 6d per day extra whilst blacksmith away, per order of Mr G. 17.9.02.

J. Wright. Driver. City Road Stables, between Lock and Tunnel. Reduced to 4/2d from 4/6d per day and no overtime payments. 6.3.03.

J. Wooley. Superintendent. Lime House Stables. Transferred to Salt Lane Lock in 1904. Wages with house 30/- per week.

II From the Minutes of the Shropshire Union Canal Company

Executive Committee, Euston Station, London, February 21 1917

Minute No 24844. Reported that the following horses had been added to the stock since the previous meeting.

Jan 1/4539. Brougham (for executive inspections) £65.

Cartage £98.

Return of horse stocktaking on 31st Dec 1916, showed 431 horses, cost £18,601 against 472 horses cost £19,708 . . . 31st Dec 1915.

Minute No 24858. Minutes of Engineers Conference, February 9 1917

20729. Engineering Boatmen. Reported that it had been arranged to allow these men 5/- per day, to include the keep of horse, while unable to work while icebound, instead of their usual 7/- per day, which includes keep of horse and assistance. The Inspectors to find the men work during the frost.

Minutes of Officers Conference, February 12 1917
22658. Horses dead to be removed from the register.
             Jan 3rd 64/4210 and No 23/489.
             Jan 25th 31/3707.

Executive Committee April 18 1917

24.870. 5 cartage horses added to the stock at an average of £95 each.
Minutes of the Officers Committee, April 10 1917
22683. Horses dead to be removed from register.
             Feb 4th No 400/6382   March 5th No 460/6471
             Feb 4th No 16/1683   March 18th No 49/4250
             Feb 24th No 10/5552
22691. Reported that the six stall stable at Etruria rented from Mr Lowndes had
             been taken over by the owner Mrs Nadin, who asks for an increase in the
             rental from 4/6d per week to 5/-.
Minutes of the Engineers Conference, April 11 1917
20769. The cost of icebreaking in the several districts during the recent frosts
             was reported to have been £690.14. 1d
             viz: Wages to staff and extra men . . £451. 1. 0d
                     War Bonus £115. 8.10d
                     Horse Hire £114. 3. 3d

Executive Committee, June 13 1917

24902. Horses added to the stock or transferred during April and May.
             April 2/4857 B £48   10/4858 B £48
             May 25/4989 B £43   31/4990 B £43
             Average cost April: £48 against £38; May: £43 against £63.10.0d.

Executive Committee, July 25 1917

24928. *Horses* Reported that the following horses had been added to the stock
             since the previous meeting.
             June   35/5031 B £52   71/5036 B £54   128/5040 B £53
                        49/5032 B £49   80/5037 B £54   130/5041 B £52
                        63/5033 B £47   100/5038 B £54   138/5042 B £49
                        64/5034 B £49   127/5039 B £55   141/5043 B £54
                        69/5035 B £53
             Average cost £52 against £38.
             A return of the horse stock of the Company taken on 30th June showed
             475 horses cost £20,015 at 30th June 1916.
24955. Reported that the following horses had been added to the stock list
             since the previous meeting.
             July   4882/9   c £105   4883/4   c £110   5096/42   B £48
                       4929/25 c £112   4884/8   c £112   5097/78   B £55
             Average cost. 4 cartage £109.15.0d against £78.15.0d
                                  2 boatage £51.10.0d against £39.10.0d
             August 5142/53   B £46   5144/95   B £54   5146/144 B £49
                       5143/71   B £46   5145/100 B £49   5146/149 B £54
                       4993/2   c £25
             Average costs. 6 Boatage £49.13.0d against £40.10.0d
                                  1 Cartage £25

24973. Applications from Inspectors for increased Expenses Allowance. The Inspectors of the Ellesmere, Norbury and Welshpool Districts have asked for an increase in the present allowance of £60 a year for keep of horses and personal expenses. The Committee gave authority for the allowance to be increased from £60 to £90 per annum.

24975. 22768. Maesbury, Canal Cartage. The Horse Superintendent considers 3 horses necessary to do the work at this station owing to the heavy cartage, and an additional horse has therefore been sent there.

Minutes of Officers Conference, February 11 1918

22823. Fatal Accident to W. Lloyd, carter, Cheshire. Reported that on December 22nd 1917, on Lloyd releasing the horse from the lorry, the animal went towards the stable, Lloyd following, and, as far as can be ascertained, the horse kicked the man into the canal. It is presumed that Lloyd was stunned as life was extinct when he was got out of the water. At the inquest a verdict of 'Accidentally drowned' was returned. £269.12.1d has been paid to the widow under the Workman's Compensation Act.

Minutes of Executive Committee, October 15 1919

25301. *Strike* Mr Whittam reports that (in connection with the strike of railway employees) the shore staff at principal depots and the majority of boatmen . . . stopped work on Saturday, Sept 26th, resuming work on Monday and Tuesday Oct 6th and 7th [the strike lasted 11 days]. Arrangements were made ensuring the horses being fed and looked after, this service in some instances being undertaken by the strikers.

III   Rules and regulations

From Rules, Bylaws, Regulations and Orders of the Navigation of the Trent and Mersey Canal, 1867

'That every person having the care of any boat or vessel upon the said Navigation shall cause the same to be drawn by one horse or mule, and not more than one at any time, except horses or mules drawing Trent Boats and Lighters, under the penalty of 20/- for every such offence.'

From notice board in Canal Museum, Stoke Bruerne

'Any captain found riding his horse or allowing others to do so will be dismissed from the Company's service.' [Probably owned by the Grand Junction Canal Company.]

From Bylaws of the Staffordshire and Worcestershire Canal Co

'7.   Boatmen, where they meet on the towing path of the canal, must drive their horses on the left side of the towing path, as is usual on turnpike roads, and the horse next the hedge, or furthest from the canal, must drop the line, in order that the horse next the canal, may pass over it.'

'8.   No boatman will be permitted to navigate without a rudder or without a competent person on board to steer (and in case of two boats hauled together, on each such boat) or without a person to attend the horse.'

'14.   No person shall ride, lead or drive any horse or other animal (not actually employed in hauling a boat) or drive or conduct any cart or other vehicle on the towing path, unless legally entitled to do so.'

Canal tunnels with towing paths

		Yards
Netherton	Birmingham Canal Navigations	3127
Chirk	Shropshire Union Canal	502
Coseley	Birmingham Canal Navigations	360
Newbold	Oxford Canal	250
Scout	Huddersfield Narrow Canal	220
Whitehouses	Shropshire Union Canal	191
Woodley	Peak Forest Canal	167
Armitage	Trent and Mersey Canal (now opened)	130
Edgbaston (Birmingham)	Worcester and Birmingham Canal	105
Hag	Cromford Canal	93
Ellesmere	Shropshire Union Canal	87
Cowley	Shropshire Union Canal	81
Knott Hill	Rochdale Canal	78
Gregory	Cromford Canal	76
Cookley	Staffordshire and Worcestershire Canal	65
Bath	Kennet and Avon Canal	59
Curdworth	Birmingham Canal Navigations	57
Bath	Kennet and Avon Canal	55

Short tunnels under 50 yards in length

Ashted	Birmingham Canal Navigations
Buckland Hollow	Cromford Canal
Sowerby Long Bridge	Rochdale Canal

Places to visit

The Waterways Museum, Stoke Bruerne, near Northampton.
Llangollen Canal Museum, Llangollen, North Wales (near Wrexham).
Exeter Maritime Museum, The Quay, Exeter, Devon.
The National Maritime Museum, Greenwich, London.
The Science Museum, South Kensington, London.
Goole Museum, Carlisle Street, Goole, Humberside.
Manchester Museum, Oxford Road, Manchester.
South Yorkshire Industrial Museum, Cusworth Hall, Doncaster.
The Black Country Museum, Dudley, Worcestershire (West Midlands).
The Ironbridge Gorge Industrial Museum, Church Hill, Ironbridge, Telford, Salop.
Morwellham Quay, near Tavistock, Devon.
The Boat Museum, Ellesmere Port, Merseyside.
Manchester Ship Canal Company Museum, Ship Canal House, King Street, Manchester. (Only to be visited on gaining permission in writing.)
Shardlow Canal Museum, Trent and Mersey Canal, (Shardlow Village), Derbyshire.
The Tiverton Museum, St Andrews Street, Tiverton, Devon.
Dunhampstead Wharf, Canal Museum, near Droitwich Spa, Worcester-Birmingham Canal, (Hereford-Worcestershire).
Canal Docks, Stourport-on-Severn, (Hereford-Worcestershire).

Glossary of terms relating to the inland waterways

I Horses and harnesses

Animal Either a donkey or towing animal of any kind. Pronounced 'hanimal' in both cases.
Baccaing Allowing a horse or mule to haul the boat unattended.
Barrel The body or ribcage of a horse, donkey or mule.
Blinkers Also known as Winkers. Leather eye shades worn by equine creatures in draught, to prevent them catching a glimpse of the following load.
Bobbins Rounded wooden members used to prevent the chafing of traces against the flanks of a horse, mule or donkey.
Brasses Horse brasses worn as a decoration and amulet. Also displayed in boat cabin interiors.
Breeching Hind-quarters of a horse and rearward parts of the harness.
Bridle System of head and face straps, worn by a horse or mule, forming attachments for bit and reins.
Browband Leather strap across the forehead of a horse, forming part of the bridle.
Chain harness Draught harness for heavy work, based on chains rather than leather straps.
Clyde Clydesdale horse. The heavy draught horse of Scotland.
Cob Short, stocky equine creature, between a horse and a pony. Can be ridden or driven. Frequently seen on the Birmingham Canal Navigations.
Collar Draught or neck collar worn by a towing animal, to which other items of harness are attached, allowing it greater purchase for hauling. In some continental countries a breast collar or harness was worn.
Confetti Tiny bits of coloured paper mixed with oats to discourage them from being stolen.
Crownpiece Leather strap worn on top of the bridle, above the poll.
Crupper Loop-strap to retain the tail of a draught horse.
Draught The ability of a towing animal to move its load. Hauling a load, and the condition of hauling. Horses kept for hauling rather than riding or pack work are known as 'draught' horses. These may be heavy draught or cart horses and light draught horses for coaches, carriages and smaller vehicles. There are also draught ponies and cobs or dual purpose animals, between a horse and pony, that may be driven and ridden.
Feather Hair or fetlock on the legs of a horse.

Feed-barrel   Barrel or similar container in which corn and bran, etc, may be kept.

Feed basket   Feed basket made of withies. Worn by a horse while feeding at its work and on the move.

Fetlock   Hair on a horses' leg, also the lower joint of the leg from which it often grows.

Forge   Place where a horse may be shod.

Gear   Canal term for the harness of a boat horse, donkey or mule.

Hames   Bars on a neck collar to which tughooks and rein rings are attached. Joined at the bottom (in pairs) by hooks and at the top by chains or straps.

Hands   The width of a man's hand, said to be an average measurement of four inches. Used in measuring the height of a horse from ground level to the withers or top of the shoulders.

Horse boy   Term mainly used on the canals of Scotland for a postillion riding a boat horse.

Horse knocker   The boy or youth in charge of towing horses on the Stour Navigations or in the Fens.

Kicking stall   Stall or standing in a stable, partitioned from the next stall.

Loose box   Enclosed, box-like stall in which a horse may be stabled. This allows much more room and freedom of movement than the kicking stall.

Martingale or False Martingale   Connecting strap worn between the forelegs of a horse, forming attachment for the breastplate.

Muzzle   The nose and mouth of a horse; protective cage worn over the nose and mouth to prevent snapping or grazing.

Nose can   Brightly painted tin-can from which a canal horse feeds while on the move. Similar to a feed basket.

Nose bowl   Wooden container from which a horse may feed while on the move. Similar to a nose can but made of wood.

Over-reach   The rear hoofs of a horse, mule or donkey accidentally striking against the forelegs.

Pony   Small horse under 14 hands high.

Postillion   Person riding a horse in draught. Frequently wore a special livery with shell-jacket and jockey cap.

Punch   The Suffolk Punch. A heavy draught horse of East Anglia.

Quarter strap   Harness strap worn across the loins.

Rollers   Alternative name for bobbins (see Bobbins).

Rosette   Flat, rounded disc-shaped ornament at the junction between browband, throatlash and cheekstraps.

Roving   Towing along the canals or rivers of the waterways' system.

Saddle   A riding saddle on which the postillion or horse boy might sit; a cart saddle or saddle-pad worn by draught horses, forming attachment for various parts of chain and strap harness.

Shire   Shire horse. Typical English heavy draught horse. Noted for its combined strength and docility, also for the large amount of feather on its legs.

Smacking whip   Whip carried by boaters, mainly for signalling purposes through cracking and smacking.

Strap harness   Harness for a light draught horse, made up of leather straps rather than chains.

Stretcher   Horizontal track-stick to which a towing line is attached.

Tackstring   The end of a towing rope or line; spare length of towing rope carried on horse boats.

Tandem Two draught animals working one behind the other.

Tassels Worn by boat horses to keep dust and flies out of their eyes.

Terrets Rings to guide reins and traces on harness.

Thong Supple, plaited cord forming connection between whip-lash and stock or handle.

Throatlash Diagonal strap of a bridle fitting under the jaw, near the junction of head and neck.

Thrums Knotted bows ornamenting a whip thong. Causes an extra loud crack.

Traces Straps, chains or cords connecting the harness of a horse with its load.

Tracking Hauling a boat or barge from the towing path.

Track-string Connection between harness and towing line or rope.

Tughook Attachment for tug chains or traces on a horse collar.

Ventholes Holes in a certain type of leather muzzle, allowing a horse, wearing the muzzle, to breathe.

Winkers Same as Blinkers (see Blinkers).

Welsh Cob Light draught horse of Welsh origins, also a dual purpose horse of great courage and strength.

II Boats and barges

Back door Communicating door between hold and cabin on a narrow boat.

Bargee Crewmen serving on a barge or lighter. Sometimes the owner-skipper of a barge.

Barge Master Skipper of a barge.

Bedhole Bed-cupboard on a canal boat, concealing a folding bed or bunk.

Benchbunk Side bunk in the stern cabin of a canal boat. Used as a seat in the daytime and as a bed at night.

Boat Captain Master or skipper of a narrow boat. Not to be confused with a bargee of barge master.

Boater Person living or working on a canal narrow boat.

Bowhaulier Person hired to haul a boat or barge from the towing path, mainly along river navigations.

Box mast Square-shaped, telescopic mast, the upper section fitting into a box or base. Used for towing purposes.

Breasting up Two or more boats secured side by side for river navigation or passing throgh wide locks.

Bulk Bulbous structure at the fore-end of a canal boat. Made of canvas stuffed with hay, merely to improve the appearance of the fore-end.

Butty First boat, when a pair of boats are towed by horses; second boat when towed by a tug.

Cabin block Wooden upright, supporting top planks on the forward part of a stern cabin.

Carvel-build Mode of boat or barge building in which side planks fit edge to edge.

Catcher Hook-like boat anchor, used when a canal boat ventures into a river or estuary.

Chalico Dressing of tar, cowhair and horse dung, used in the construction of wooden canal boats.

Clinker-build Boat building with overlapping side planks. More suitable for rougher waters than carvel-built, or smooth-sided craft.

Cockpit Entrance to the rear part of a stern cabin. A step-down or well-deck.

Composite boat Canal boat made of iron or steel with a wooden bottom.

Counter The flat, rounded stern of certain types of craft.

Cratch Near triangular frontboard on a narrow boat and the frame-like structure by which it is supported.

Crock cupboard Corner cupboard in a boat cabin, with shelves on which china is displayed. The front of the cupboard lets down in the form of a table.

Cuddy North Country term for a barge or boat cabin.

Deck lid Hinged hatch or cover above the fore-cabin or rope locker on a narrow boat.

Elum Combined tiller and rudder post of a canal boat.

Family boat Working boat on which the crew is a man and his wife and/or family.

Fender Buffer of coiled rope-ends, used on a boat or barge to prevent ramming against a wharf or lockside.

Fore cabin The bow or forward cabin on a boat or barge. Sometimes used as a rope locker or place of storage.

Gunwale The upper line of a craft, especially down the sides. Pronounced 'gunnel'. This was the position from which guns were fired on armed merchantmen.

Hatches Covers over a hold or cargo space; cockpit or well-deck on a boat or barge, and doors leading from cockpit to cabin.

Joey Boater Crewman of a 'Joey' or day boat.

Keelson Inner or false keel of a boat or barge, to which ribs may be attached. Runs the full length of the craft from stem to stern.

Lock wheeler Person running or riding ahead of a canal boat to open the next lock.

Long bottoms Longtitudinal wooden planks used in the construction of certain canal craft.

Mast box The lower section of a box-mast, containing the upper or telescopic section. This is raised for towing purposes when the boat is low in the water.

Measham ware Ornamental tea sets, collected and used by boaters and their families. Noted for its dark brown glaze and coloured motifs.

Monkey box Locker or box in which cleaning materials and old rags are kept, on a boat or barge.

Navigation lamp Oil lamp carried on the frontboard of a narrow boat. Used in tunnels.

Navvies Short for navigators. Originally men constructing or working on the line of a canal.

Number-one An owner-boater.

Owner-boater The owner and master of a boat on which he also lives and works.

Ram's head Rudder post of a narrow boat or barge.

Rims Brass rims or rings ornamenting the stove pipe of a narrow boat. Seldom seen in the north of England.

Rodney Boater Careless individual keeping an untidy boat. A slum-dweller of the inland waterways.

Running blocks Wooden blocks on the tops of stands or uprights, through which a towing line might be guided-out.

Shadowgraph   Lettering on narrow boats and barges, showing either the name of the craft or its owner. This is given an almost three-dimensional effect by means of shading and outlining. First used on farm wagons and carts.

Shafting   Poling or punting a boat or barge with a boat shaft.

Shearings   Oak panels lining the interior of a canal boat.

Side cloths   Protective canvas covers over the cargo space of a canal boat.

Slackboards   Also known as washboards. Long, flat boards, roped together, intended to raise the sides of canal boats to prevent water washing inboard.

Slide   Hatch cover, especially over the cockpit of a narrow boat stern cabin.

Stern cabin   Rearmost living cabin on a canal narrow boat.

Stretchers   Cross members used to strengthen the overall structure of a canal boat.

Tiller   Curved or straight beam used for steering a canal craft. Reversed at night-time when a boat reaches its final moorings.

Top planks   Gangway or footway on a canal boat, above the cargo space. Extends from cabin to cratch, supported by masts, struts and stands.

Towing post   Mast used for towing purposes.

Tumblehome   Inward sloping sides of a living cabin on a canal boat.

Tunnel cutter   Metal loop or ring above the aperture of a stove pipe, used to disperse smoke in a tunnel and to guard the chimney from falling leaves or—in a tunnel—from soot and plaster, etc.

Turk's Head   Woven cordage or ropework, binding the top of the rudder or ram's head on a narrow boat.

Washboards   Same as slackboards (see Slackboards).

Windlass   Drum-shaped spindle with cranked handles used for raising an anchor (appears on the foredecks of certain barges); L-shaped handle used in opening the paddles on lock gates.

Windlass hole   Cupboard in the stern cabin of a narrow boat, in which a spare L-shaped windlass is kept.

Bibliography

A Home Tour through the manufacturing districts of England in the Summer of 1835, Sir George Head, Frank Cass & Co Ltd, 1968.

Bradshaw's Canals and Navigable Rivers, 1904, H. de Salis, reprinted by David and Charles, 1966.

Narrow Boat, L.T.C. Rolt, Eyre and Spottiswood, 1944.

The Inland Waterways of England, L.T.C. Rolt, George Allen and Unwin, 1950.

British Canals, Charles Hadfield, David and Charles, 1966.

The Heavy Horse, its Harness and Harness Description, Terry Keegan, 1970.

The Canaller's Bedside Book, John Gagg, David and Charles, 1973.

Canal Boats and Boaters, D.J. Smith, Hugh Evelyn, 1973.

Discovering Craft of the Inland Waterways, D.J. Smith, Shire Publications Ltd, 1977.

Narrow Boat Painting, A.J. Lewery, David and Charles, 1974.

The Complete Book of Canal and River Navigations, Edward W. Paget-Tomlinson, Waine Research Publications, 1978.

Staffordshire and Worcestershire Canal (Towpath Guide No 1), J. Ian Langford, Goose and Son, 1974.

Magazines

Riding Annual, 1978. Article by D.J. Smith.

Journal of the Railway and Canal Historical Society.

Waterways News.

Waterways World.

Canal and Riverboat Monthly.

Transport History (Quarterly).

Index

Other Titles of Interest

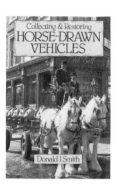
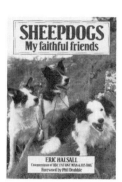

Collecting and Restoring Horse-drawn Vehicles

by Donald J. Smith

This is more than a nostalgic glance at a bygone age, it is also a useful and practical guide for all who would like to acquire a horse-drawn vehicle or enjoy the pastime of preserving one.

In preparation

A View of Nature

by Christopher Parsons

1982 sees the 25th anniversary of the founding of the BBC Natural History Unit, whose films, such as *Life on Earth*, have won international acclaim. Their cameras have filmed world-wide, recording the earth's wildlife and championing its preservation. Christopher Parsons, the Head of the Unit, tells many amusing and fascinating anecdotes about these expeditions and about the many personalities involved, including Gerald Durrell, Sir Peter Scott and David Attenborough.

Working Dogs

by Joan Palmer

This book explores the many roles which dogs play in today's society, from those used to help advertise or promote goods to racing dogs, game dogs, security dogs and tracker dogs engaged in mountain rescue work.

Sheepdogs: My faithful friends

by Eric Halsall

Foreword by Phil Drabble

Having brought the excitement of sheepdog trials to the viewers of the BBC television series, *One Man and His Dog*, Eric Halsall describes the working collie and its life, breeding, training, work and history for the delight of all country lovers.

Sheepdog trials

by Eric Halsall

Trials are more than sheepdog competitions for competition's sake: they are a means by which shepherds select the best dogs in order to improve the overall breed. Eric Halsall outlines, in language for the layman, how a trial is judged, pointing out what the judges are looking for, and gives the public many fascinating background details about the team work of the dogs and men on their home farms.

Buying and Renovating a Cottage

by Stuart Turner

This is the ideal handbook for anyone contemplating the purchase or restoration of an old cottage. Written in a humorous, yet down to earth style, by a man who has already restored several cottages and knows the pitfalls well, it will certainly appeal to the do-it-yourself handyman.

A maintenance craft (converted narrow boat), Shropshire Union Canal, 1956